DESERT art

THE DESART DIRECTORY OF CENTRAL AUSTRALIAN ABORIGINAL ART AND CRAFT CENTRES

Compiled by Mary-Lou Nugent for Desart:
the Association of Central Australian Aboriginal Art and Craft Centres

jukurrpa books

First published in 1998 by **jukurrpa books**,
an imprint of IAD Press
PO Box 2531
Alice Springs NT 0871
Ph: 08-8951 1311
Fax: 08-8952 2527

Reprinted in 2000

National Library of Australia Catalogue-in-Publication data:

Desert art: the Desart directory of Central Australian Aboriginal art and craft centres.

ISBN 1 86465 004 4.

1. Aborigines, Australian – Australia, Central – Art – Directories. 2. Art centres – Australia, Central – Directories. I. Nugent, Mary-Lou, 1960– . II. Desart Inc.

704.039915

Compiled by Mary-Lou Nugent
Designed by Christine Bruderlin
Photography by Barry Skipsey, unless otherwise credited
Map by Brenda Thornley
Printed in Australia by Gillingham Printers

ATSIC

Desart gratefully acknowledges the financial assistance of the Aboriginal and Torres Strait Islander Commission.

Foreword

Inawinytji Williamson

Walka-tjarangkula aṟa tjuṯa mulapa utiṉi, walka puḻka tjuṯangku nganananya tjukaruru tjuṯanya utiṟa nintilpai, nganampa walytjapitiku Tjukurpa walkatjarangku nintilpai uṉtalpiti, katjapiṯi, kamipiṯi munu tjamupiṯi. Walka tjuṯanya nganampa kaltjawanu puḻka mulapa tjungu ngaṟanyi. Nganana artwork art centre-ngka palyantjanyala kutjupa-kutjupa way-ngku palyaṉi. Palu nganana artwork kutjupa-kutjupa way-ngku palyantjangku utiṉi, Aṉangungku easy way-ngku aṟa tjukurpa-tjaranya munu iriṯi nyinantjatjaranya puṉu piṟanpa-tjangurungku wiṟuṟa palyaṉi. Walka tjuṯanya iriṯi mantangka munu pulingka walkatjunkupai kutju munu iriṯi tjamupiṯingku munu kamipiṯingku tjanampa tjitji tjuṯakutu aṟa mantangka walkatjunkula tjakultjunkupai. Walka tjuṯa tjukuritja tjuṯangku Aṉangu tjuṯaku nintiṟa unngu. Walka tjutangku Tjukurpa nintilpai yaaltji-yaaltji panya iriṯi nyinantja munu walkangkuya utiṟa nintiṉi yaaltji-yaaltji Aṉangu tjuṯa kuwari, tjukaruru wiṟuṟa nyinantjaku. Walkangku utiṟa nintiṉi wati, minyma yangupala tjuṯakutu panya tjilpi munu pampa tjuṯaku aṟa munu Tjukurpa puḻka tjuṯanya yangupala tjuṯangku nyakula, kuliṟa nintiringkuntjaku. Aṟa puḻka tjuṯaya tjilpingku munu pampangku kanyiṉi aṟa panya walytja tjuṯaku ngura walytjatjara.

Wiṟu alatjiṯu ngaṟanyi waakaringkula nintiringkuntjaku, pampa munu minyma yangupala tjutanyaya art centre-ngka tjunguringkula waakaringanyi. Art centre-ngka minyma yangupala tjutangkuya kuntili pampa tjuṯanguru ninti-ringkunyangka wati yangupala tjuṯangkuya nintiringanyi tjanapa kamuṟunguṟu munu tjamunguṟu. Puḻka alatjiṯu ngaṟanyi tjitji nganampa tjuṯaku palya wiṟuṟa pitjala art centre-ngka nyakula ninti-ringkuntjaku tjanampa walytja tjuṯangku art waaka palyannyangka.

Nganana kuliṉi walka tjuṯanyala palyantjanya bridge puṟunypa ngaṟanyi. Aṉangu tjuṯanguru piṟanpa tjuṯakutu, nganampa walka tjuṯa-tjarangkula utiṟa nintini piṟanpa tjuṯanya nganampa kaltjaku munu aṟa tjuṯaku. Walka tjuṯangku nintini yaaltji-yaaltji Aṉangu tjuṯanyala kuwari nyinanyi. Munula nintini yaaltji-yaaltjingku puṉu palyantjaku panya wira tjuṯa munu kuḻaṯa. Kutjupala fabric-angka utiṟa wangkanyi inmaku pakantjatjara, kukaku munu maiku ankuntjatjara munu inma tjuṯatjara.

Aṟa kutjara puḻka mulapa ngaṟanyi nampa kutju piṟanpangku kulintjaku nganampa ngura walytja yaaltjingka ngaṟanyi munu aṟa panya nganana Tjukurpa-nguṟu utiringkuntja. Kutjupa ngaṟanyi puḻka mulapa panya Aṉangu kutjupa-tjarangku munu piṟanpa tjuṯangku nyanga-tjanampa nintiringkuntjaku. Tjanampa ngaṟanyi palya nintiringkuntjaku nganampa Tjukurpaku munu kaltjaku. Nganana tjananya nganampa Tjukurpaku munu kaltjaku nintiṉi palulanguru tjana ngananananya tjukarurungku wiṟuṟa kulilku nganampa way tjuṯaku.

Community winkingkuya puḻkaṟa pukularinganyi art centre tjuṯaku munuya mukuringanyi art centre tjuṯanya tiṯutjara ngaṟakatintjaku. Art centre-nguṟungku Aṉanguku Tjukurpa utilkatinyangkaya Aṉangu tjuṯangku ngurkantananyi tjanampa Tjukurpa. Art centre tjutanyaya wiṟu alatjiṯu art centre tjuṯanguṟungkumaṉtu Aṉanguku kaltja puḻkaṟa wiṟuṟa tjukarurungku atunymananyi munu utilkatinyi. Alatji ngaṟanyi waaka nganmantjatjanya nyakula wangkapai palatja tjukarurungku palyantjawiya

munu palulangu_rungku wangkara wi_ru_ra pi_rukungku tjukaru_ru_ra kutjupankupai.

Pu_lka mulapa nga_ranyi art centre tju_tanya ti_tutjarangku kanyintjaku. Art centre tju_tangkulanya alpamila_ra A_nanguku kaltja walka tju_tawanungku nintilkatinyi. Tjingu_rula wiya art centrengka waakaringanyi alatjingkala pu_tu kulilku wi_ru_ra tjitji ma_latja tju_tanya nintilkatintjikitjangku, kaltja nganampa. A_nangu artist tju_tangkuya art centre tju_tanya run-amila_ni munuya pi_ranpa co-ordinator kanyi_ni tjananya alpamilantjaku art centre-ngka. Art centre, walytjangku A_nangungku run-mila_ra ku_npungku wi_ru_ra art munu craft palyantja tju_tanya sell-amila_ni.

Nyangangka ngana_na Desart-wanu munu community kutjupa tju_tawanu waakaringanyi. Community wangka kutjupa kutjupa tju_ta-wanula waakaringanyi wangka panya — Pitjantjatjara, Eastern Arrernte, Western Arrernte, Luritja, Pintupi, Warlpiri, Anmatyerr munu Warumungu — A_nangu wangka kutjupa-kutjupala wi_ru_ra watarku waakaringanyi. Ngana_na tjunguringkula wi_ru_ra warkaringkuntjangku A_nangu uwankaranya kutju_ra ku_npuni. Kutjuringkulanyangka ku_npuringkupai. Palya!

Art is part of our expression, it's a part of our values, it's all our families' history which is being passed on to our children. It's our culture and it's part of our lives, and not separate to it. The artwork made in our art centres is very different at the different art centres. But it all shows how people can adapt their stories and histories to suit new ways of working. The designs come from stories in the sand and from our grandmothers and grandfathers telling the stories to the young children. The pictures come from the Tjukurpa also. They tell about the old days and they teach people how to live today. The art tells young people today about what the older people know. It's very important and tells them where their family comes from.

It's good to work and learn, the older women and younger women are coming together and working in these centres. Here they can learn from the elders, they learn from watching their aunties while the young men learn from their uncles and grandfathers. It's important for our grandchildren to come in and be able to watch and learn from their older relations doing this work.

We see that our art is like a bridge between non-Aboriginal people and Aboriginal people, making them aware of our culture and stories. Our paintings tell non-Aboriginal people about how we live. We can show them how we use artefacts such as coolamons and spears, and how, on our fabric, we can talk about the dancing, hunting and ceremonies.

It's not just important for our people to see where we belong and to know where we come from through the Tjukurpa, it's also important for people from outside to know about these things. They can learn about the Tjukurpa and about our culture, making people aware of what our values and our beliefs are.

The communities are very supportive of these centres and they would like to see them continue. The work that is made shows a record of the Tjukurpa, and people can see it and recognise that it's their own Tjukurpa. The centres are a good way of ensuring that cultural activities are maintained and done the proper way. If you look back and see that something wasn't done properly you can talk about it and change it.

It's important to keep these centres strong. They provide us with a way of passing on our culture through our artwork. If we were not able to work through the centres, the process of passing on knowledge from generation to generation will become more difficult and may weaken. These centres are managed by Aboriginal artists who employ Aboriginal and non-Aboriginal coordinators. It is through these centres that we can control what happens with our work.

Here, through Desart, we work together with other communities from all around this area. It doesn't matter what language they speak — Pitjantjatjara, Eastern Arrernte, Western Arrernte, Luritja, Pintupi, Warlpiri, Anmatyerr and Warumungu — all the people are working together to keep this going. As we help one another, it makes us a whole body. We stick together — when you become as one, you become strong. *Palya!*

Inawinytji Williamson
Director of Desart, 1997

Foreword

Gatjil Djerrkura

It gives me great pleasure to introduce this important resource.

Indigenous arts and crafts do far more to provide Australia with a distinct international cultural identity than most other creative works. The international and domestic appetite for indigenous arts and crafts continues to grow. If the prices paid at recent auctions are indicators, serious collectors of traditional art forms are advised to get in well before the Olympic Games.

With this growing interest, it is important for our communities to ensure that the creators of the works receive appropriate recognition and remuneration; the arts and crafts industry is one of the few culturally relevant ways for Aboriginal people, especially on remote communities, to access the Western economic system.

Community-based art and craft centres in Central Australia have proven themselves as the key to the development of both Aboriginal identity and economic opportunity. They do more than market the cultural products of Aboriginal people, they also maintain links with traditional country, provide materials, assist with essential documentation, offer advice on copyright and contracts and provide management skills.

While the marketing role is significant, these other social and cultural activities are important because they safeguard the elements that are unique to Aboriginal art — the elements that make them so attractive to visitors and major collectors.

With this in mind, I believe that resources such as this directory have a vital role to play in helping the different sectors of the industry — artists and creators, agents and purchasers — to get in touch with each other. It is essential that each sector understands and respects the needs of each other, and that each understands the protocols that are necessary for satisfactory transactions.

I wish to congratulate Desart for its initiative in producing this resource. I commend this book to anyone with a stake in the arts and crafts of Central Australia.

Gatjil Djerrkura OAM
Chairman, Aboriginal and Torres Strait Islander Commission

Contents

Acknowledgments

Desart would like to thank its staff involved in the production of this catalogue: Project Coordinator Mary-Lou Nugent; Ron Brien, Amelia Forrester and Geraldine Tyson; the Desart Executive; Inawinytji Williamson and Beverley Peacock of Kaltjiti Arts and Crafts; Mrs Wallace and Tim Rollason of Keringke Arts; Elaine Namatjira, Carol Rontji and Naomi Sharp of Hermannsburg Potters; Valerie Cullinan and Cheryl Hawkins-Clarke of Iwantja Arts and Crafts; and Bessie Liddle and Sandra Rounsevell-Aidon of Jukurrpa Artists Corporation.

The following artists and art centre staff supplied information and helped in the production of this catalogue: Marlene Power and Jo-Anne Rankin, Ali Curung Women's Centre; Geoffrey Shannon, Anne Schofield, and Tony Jefferies, Anyinginyi Congress; Nyukana Baker and Louise Partos, Ernabella Arts Inc.; Daisy Napaltjarri Jugadai, Narputta Nangala and Marina Strocchi, Ikuntji Women's Centre; Nikki Morrison, Trish Dobson and Alison Alder, Julalikari Council CDEP Women's Art and Craft Programme; Janis Stanton and Daphne Williams, Papunya Tula Artists Pty Ltd; Rene Douglas, Lena Campbell and Linda Herangi, Titjikala Women's Centre; Lena Apwerl and Jan Ross Manley, Utopia Cultural Centre and Utopia Awely Batik Aboriginal Corporation; Gay English and Dahlia Abdel-Aziz, Walkatjara Art Centre; Gary Proctor and Albie Vegas, Warburton Arts Project; Samson Japaljarri Martin, Uni Nampijinpa Martin, Andrea Nungarrayi Martin and Susan Congreve, Warlukurlangu Artists Aboriginal Association; Alison Anderson and Liz Teper, Warumpi Arts; Perry Japanangka Langdon and Dale McCauley, Yurrampi Crafts; Gordon Inkatji and Steve Fox, Maruku Arts and Crafts.

Thanks also to Flick Wright, Kolokuwi; Christine Lennard; Jennifer Isaacs; Norm Wilson at ATSIC; Penny Watson at Batchelor College; Marg Bowman at Jukurrpa Books; Christine Bruderlin; and Dianne James, project coordinator for the first Desart catalogue.

Interpretive assistance has been given by Lorna Wilson, Kamiku Arangku; Therese Ryder and Liesl Rockchild, Santa Teresa; and Lizzie Ellis helped with the Western Desert languages.

Desart gratefully acknowledges the financial assistance of the Aboriginal and Torres Strait Islander Commission.

Preface

Desert Art is the second review by Desart, an independent association of Aboriginal art and craft centres of Central Australia, of the work of its members.

Desart is an ATSIC-funded organisation, initiated and controlled by the Aboriginal-owned art and craft centres of Central Australia. These centres, in turn, support approximately four thousand Aboriginal artists and craftspeople, most of whom live on remote communities and homelands dotted around a vast area. Prior to incorporation in April 1992, Desart was known as the Central Australian Aboriginal Arts Industry Support Unit.

The primary role of the association is to provide industry-specific information, advice and practical assistance to Aboriginal art centres in the region. Desart acts as an important reference point for government departments and agencies, arts organisations and agents as well as those with an interest in cultural tourism. By disseminating information as widely as possible and offering advice and guidance to those with an academic or commercial interest in Central Australian Aboriginal art and craft, Desart aims to promote and facilitate sustainable growth in the industry for the future.

Desart is, in effect, the collective voice of the Aboriginal art centres of Central Australia, working towards coordinated development, support and strong representation for Aboriginal art and craft producers.

Desart has collected information for *Desert Art* from the artists and staff of each art and craft centre. A 1993 publication covered the 12 art centres then in operation in Central Australia. In this catalogue the work of 19 centres is featured. There are, however, more emerging art centres in the region; it is anticipated that these will be included in future Desart publications.

Individual centres have chosen to include mention of particular artists where they have been involved with the development of the centre, where they have been involved in exhibitions, commissions or projects, or where their individual work has directly influenced the direction of the centre. There are, however, many other artists who work through each of these art centres and their work is equally significant. A more detailed list of artists is available by contacting each centre directly. Contact details are listed at the back of this book.

MN

Tjukurpa

The 'Tjukurpa', or 'Dreamtime' or 'Dreaming' as it is sometimes loosely translated into English, is fundamental to Central Australian Aboriginal life. It defines traditional Aboriginal law and religion and encompasses the land and its creation and all that exists. Different language groups of the Centre have different words and spellings for the same concept, sometimes capitalised and sometimes not. Some of these are: Tjukurpa (Pitjantjatjara language), Altyerre (Arrernte), Jukurrpa (Warlpiri) and Tjukurrpa (Pintupi-Luritja).

What are Aboriginal art and craft centres?

The Aboriginal art and craft centres of Central Australia are non-profit associations whose members are Aboriginal artists and craftspeople. The majority of these centres are represented by Desart, a resource and advocacy organisation funded by the Aboriginal and Torres Strait Islander Commission. Some art and craft centres are situated in urban areas but over half of them are located more than 300 km from Alice Springs in remote Aboriginal communities stretching across the Northern Territory, Western Australia and South Australia.

The main focus of centres is to encourage the production of art and craft by their members and assist those artists who wish to sell and market their work. As well as this, the centres provide a range of services to their members, their local communities and others. They record traditional stories and document artworks in a wide variety of media (photographs, tape, video, film and print). They act as a contact point for visitors whose interests may be academic, curatorial or business related, frequently providing information and guided tours. Many art and craft centres provide support for funerals and ceremonies and to members during times of crisis. A number of centres coordinate bush trips for artists and support cultural activities. Art and craft centres coordinate exhibitions and arrange travel for participating artists. They are a resource for other community organisations, often helping to print posters and T-shirts, donating paintings for fundraising or helping with local school activities. Art and craft centres license designs for commercial reproduction and process copyright requests for, and on behalf of, artists. Some centres produce value-added products such as cards and postcards, while others are involved in the establishment and maintenance of community museums.

Art and craft centres provide a meeting place. They encourage the training of younger artists and they arrange trainers and workshops, creating opportunities for artists to learn new techniques and experiment with different media. The centres provide employment and training opportunities for local people in the management of an art centre. They provide training in office-bearer and executive responsibilities for their management committees which, in turn, ensures greater control by artists.

Art coordinators are fundamental to the success of many art centres in Central Australia. Many of the above functions and activities are carried out by the coordinator and their efforts, energy and vision continue to be vital influences on the evolution and management of art and craft centres.

Aboriginal art and craft centres' primary activity is the production and marketing of locally produced art and craft. However, in fulfilling this role they serve as a cultural focus for the community and answer important social, cultural maintenance and educational functions. All activities conducted by art and craft centres are underpinned by traditional Aboriginal law and culture; through these centres the Aboriginal identity is further defined and celebrated.

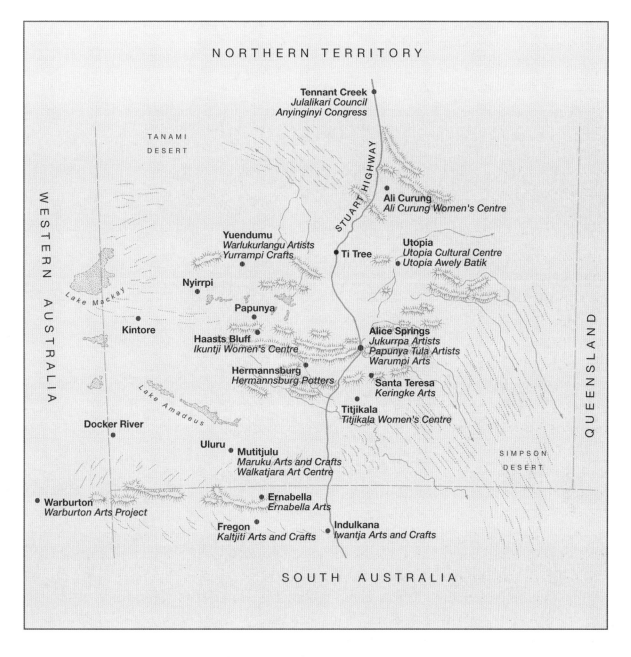

MAP SHOWING LOCATION OF CENTRAL AUSTRALIAN ABORIGINAL ART AND CRAFT CENTRES

ARTISTS AT WORK AT THE ALI CURUNG WOMEN'S CENTRE
SURROUNDED BY POTS OF VIBRANT DESERT COLOURS.

Ali Curung Women's Centre

Stories passed from one generation to the next underlie the imagery of the artwork produced at the Ali Curung Women's Centre. Warumungu, Warlpiri, Kaytetye and Alyawarr women work side by side at the Centre producing painting, jewellery and clothing in the warm colours of the surrounding desert.

The 500-strong community of Ali Curung, formerly called Warrabri, is just south of the Devils Marbles, about 380 km north-east of Alice Springs in the southern Barkly region of the Northern Territory. The Women's Centre, known locally as Arleheyarenge, started in 1995 when a previous women's centre moved into the renovated old Ali Curung clinic building. A garden of fruit trees, shrubs and lawn has been established around the centre and, nowadays, about 20 women work there, with about 10 older women coming in to paint occasionally.

All of the artists produce Central Desert-style acrylic paintings on canvas. Different family groups paint their own Dreaming stories, drawing on the imagery used in ceremonial body designs. These stories, translated to acrylic on canvas, help keep the artists' culture alive. Artists paint in natural ochre colours, adjusting them to create the hot desert colours. There are different stories for each season of the year.

While many Ali Curung women paint, others make decorative hand-painted jewellery and ornaments. Recently, successful workshops have been run at the Centre in silk painting and screenprinting. Along with the production of artwork, they sew clothes for themselves and their children.

Art and craft items from Ali Curung are sold

I've been working here since 1982. We started with a training workshop in sewing, cooking and literacy, and in 1985 I went to Alice Springs and saw the people doing dot painting. I brought the ideas back here to our community and that's how we started working. The Education Department ran workshops in silk painting and silk-screen-printing. We've been doing a lot of work for the Desert Harmony Festival in Tennant Creek. I've also got experience through adult education courses.

It's a good centre for this community, the women are proud of this place. We have a women's shelter here also. The women want to learn their history and tell the young girls about their Dreaming. They need to know about the right Dreaming to paint, like Rain Dreaming or bushtucker, about skin names and about the right stories. Through the painting and their artwork they can learn about the country and about our culture this way. They are also learning how to sew and how to make clothes for their kids. The community is proud of this centre too.

Emily Nangala Rankin

TOP: MARLENE NAPANANGKA PRESLEY, RAYLEEN NAPALJARRI CARR AND GAIL NAMPIJINPA RANKIN WITH THEIR WORK.
LEFT: GAIL NAMPIJINPA RANKIN WORKS ON A WOODEN PLATE.

in tourist outlets in Alice Springs, Darwin and Adelaide. Ali Curung artists have exhibited at the Araluen Centre in Alice Springs, at the Desert Harmony Festival in Tennant Creek and the Telstra Aboriginal Art Award in Darwin. In 1997 they held their first solo exhibition in Adelaide at the 'Desert Dwellers Aboriginal Art and Culture Centre'. While in Adelaide for the opening of this exhibition, they completed a large mural at St Paul's Church and retreat. Paintings produced at the Kaltya Business Conference at the Northern Territory University in August 1996 were recently displayed as part of a large mural entitled 'Meeting Place' and shown in Darwin for Expo '97 in the State Square at Parliament House.

Artists who work through the Ali Curung Women's Centre include: Jessie Nungarrayi Camphoo, Raylene Carr, Dorothy Napurrurla Dixon, Mona Nungarrayi Haywood, Ellen Nampijinpa Haywood, Eliza Nampijinpa Haywood, Renita Napurrurla Kelly, Judy Nampijinpa Long, Nancy Nungarrayi Long, Rene Nungarrayi Long, Virginia Nungarrayi Poulson, Marlene Napanangka Presley, Eva Napanangka Presley, Anne Marie Apetyarr Peterson, Joanne Napaljarri Rankin, Emily Nangala Rankin, Gail Nampijinpa Rankin, Joylene Nangala Robertson, May Nampijinpa Wilson and Geraldine Napangardi Riley.

Anyinginyi Congress
Arts and Cultural Gallery

J ust off the wide dusty main street of Tennant Creek in the Northern Territory is an impressive exhibition space showing the work of the Aboriginal people of the surrounding Barkly region. The Anyinginyi Congress Arts and Cultural Gallery has been operating for just two years, but this art and craft centre is already an important part of the local community.

The Gallery is a vital arm of the Anyinginyi Congress which provides quality health care for the Aboriginal people of the area. The Congress was established in 1985 after a lengthy lobbying process by local Aboriginal people. Over the past twelve years Anyinginyi Congress has been upgraded and improved and now employs over 60, mainly Aboriginal, people. Although primarily a medical centre, it takes a holistic approach to lifestyle issues and has programmes in such areas as sport and recreation, an Alcohol After Care Programme, health worker education and, of course, arts and crafts.

There are about 3500 people living in Tennant Creek; about half the population is made up of Aboriginal people, mostly from the Warumungu language group. The Arts and Cultural Gallery provides these residents, as well as the broader Aboriginal population of the Barkly region, with the opportunity to become involved in cultural pursuits through a well-equipped wood workshop and training area adjoining the Gallery. People from all backgrounds visit, watch or take an active part in learning how to carve or make wooden artefacts; a separate area is used for women to make ceramics, and jewellery from local seeds.

WOODEN ARTEFACTS GLOW IN THE AFTERNOON LIGHT.

Activities are aimed at re-establishing people's ties with their country and include going on bush trips with Aboriginal elders. On these trips people learn about bushtucker, bush medicine, and about the woods used for making traditional hunting implements such as spears, boomerangs, woomeras and digging sticks.

Paintings by local artists living in Tennant Creek, such as Willy Riley Japanangka and Rosie Riley, are sold through the Gallery. Anyinginyi Gallery also represents artists such as Betty Finlay Nakamarra, Kathleen Jackson Nungarrayi, Amy Martin Nakamarra, Louis Martin

Nakamarra and Lena Nakamarra. The work of these artists includes large and small canvas paintings in the Central Desert style, coolamons, digging sticks, *ininti* (bean tree) bead jewellery and wooden carvings.

Artwork produced at the Anyinginyi Congress art and craft centre is also sold further afield in retail gallery outlets in Alice Springs, Adelaide and Perth and across the Northern Territory. The Gallery is in the process of developing into a keeping place for local traditional and contemporary artwork and already constitutes a significant collection of work in many media from across the Barkly region.

Anyinginyi Arts is about community involvement and ownership of the sale of our art. At present we have a workshop where local people, young and old, come to make traditional artefacts like spears, boomerangs, coolamons, shields and nulla nullas, and also to sit and talk about country and culture. In this way the younger people are taught the ways of traditional culture.

This is also important to us because it explains to tourists from Australia and overseas that our culture is still alive and healthy. As well as making these things at the Gallery workshop, people go out bush and collect wood, seeds and all the other things we need, including bushtucker and bush medicine.

Dayday Frank Jakamarra

THIS PAGE, TOP: DAYDAY FRANK JAKAMARRA CAREFULLY SHAPES A PIECE OF MULGA.

LEFT: A SELECTION OF PAINTINGS PRODUCED AT ANYINGINYI CONGRESS ON DISPLAY IN THE GALLERY.

OPPOSITE PAGE, TOP: *ININTI* (BEAN TREE) SEED JEWELLERY DISPLAYED IN ANYINGINYI CONGRESS GALLERY.

LEFT: SILK SCARF BY ALISON M. CARROLL, 90 cm x 90 cm.

BELOW: COLOURFUL HAND-PAINTED ERNABELLA

JEWELLERY RESTING ON SILK; FOREGROUND SILK SCARF

HAND-PAINTED BY YILPI MICHAEL.

Ernabella Arts Inc.

As early as the 1940s Ernabella Arts has acted as a focus for Pitjantjatjara artists. It is the longest continually running Aboriginal art and craft centre in Central Australia and its influence has reached throughout the region.

Ernabella is 440 km south-west of Alice Springs, just below the Northern Territory border in South Australia. The community, established in 1937 as a Presbyterian Mission, and the surrounding homelands are home to approximately 400 Pitjantjatjara people. In the early days the mission produced spun and woven blankets and rugs, but today Ernabella Arts has an international reputation for the production of a range of fine arts and crafts. Currently its artists are producing batik and silk-screen-printed fabric lengths, acrylic paintings on canvas, soft furnishings, jewellery, prints on paper, silk paintings, carvings and ceramics.

Batik, one of the high-profile products of Ernabella Arts, was first introduced to the area in the mid-1970s. It provided a perfect means of translating the distinctive flowing imagery of Ernabella paintings from paper onto radiant silks and cottons. The batik and, more recently, silk-screen-printed fabrics, with their unique designs have become a trademark of the area. The unusual fluid symbols have developed from the traditional iconography used in the Aboriginal custom of *milpatjunanyi*, the telling of stories by drawing in the sand. Fabric lengths, often up to 4 m long, are constructed like maps of the surrounding country, with a symmetrical arrangement of motifs running across the flowing surface of the cloth, intricately connected by delicate patterning.

A dynamic colour palette typifies Ernabella textiles. Years of experience and an extensive technical knowledge have given the batik artists of the area a great control over the colours they employ. They have developed a range of rich natural browns, ochres and golds, greens, violets, brilliant reds and yellows. The batik process is a complicated one but their fabrics display the delicate balance that can be achieved when mastery of technique is married to traditional imagery and a vivid colour range. Some of Ernabella's best-known batik artists, Nyukana Baker, Atipalku Intjalki and Angkuna Kulyuru, have work held in collections throughout the world.

Screen-printing is a recent development for Ernabella and uses the same imagery of the *milpatjunanyi* in striking reds, blues and golds on dark or vividly coloured backgrounds. A purpose-built screen-printing studio has been established next to the Ernabella Arts craft room where artists, in particular Marie Warren, Nyuwara Tapaya and Vera Williams, have produced multiple repeat runs of fabric in up to eight different colour combinations. The finished fabric is often made up into soft furnishings such as chair covers, doona covers and pillowcases.

Painting on canvas began in Ernabella in the mid-1980s. Printmaking came a little later, but its introduction has been a great success. Etchings and lithographs produced by Ernabella artists at workshops at educational institutions and printmaking workshops around Australia have produced a remarkable range of limited edition prints. Prints by Nyuwara Tapaya, Nyukana Baker, Jillian Davey, Alison M. Carroll and Elsie Taylor, also renowned textile artists, have been

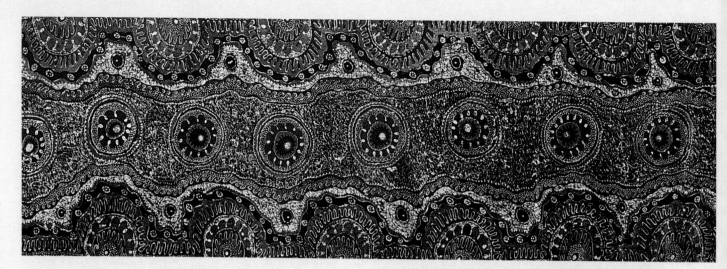

widely exhibited in major printmaking awards since 1993. Much of the inspiration for prints and painted canvases comes from body-painting designs used in traditional ceremonies associated with the Tjukurpa. Nowadays, artists are also incorporating more realistic representations of bush foods and animals to tell the stories of their country.

Ernabella art is now included in the collections of all major galleries in Australia. In 1991 one of Ernabella's younger artists, Tjalumi Kulyuru, won the Open Media Section of the National Aboriginal and Torres Strait Islander Award. In 1992 a piece by Tjunkaya Tapaya was selected for 'Lizards, Snakes and Cattledogs', an exhibition of contemporary Australian textiles held in Krefeld, Germany. Ernabella artists have exhibited in major exhibitions in Indonesia, USA and Latin America and they have travelled to Indonesia, Japan and Kenya and around Australia, accompanying their work, demonstrating their practice and running workshops.

In 1997 a ceramic collaboration was initiated with the Jam Factory Craft and Design Centre of Adelaide. Ernabella Arts is also currently, in 1998, involved in an extensive national and international exhibition and residency programme to celebrate its fiftieth anniversary.

TOP: CREPE-BACKED SILK-SATIN BATIK LENGTH, *ATIPALKU INTJALKI*, 3.2 m LENGTH.

MIDDLE: COTTON FABRICS SIDE BY SIDE; *PUTI (BUSH)*, DESIGNED BY NYUWARA TAPAYA AND NYUKANA BAKER AND PRINTED BY MARIE WARREN.

BOTTOM: *INA WIYA*, THREE-COLOUR LITHOGRAPH BY ALISON M. CARROLL, 41 cm x 31 cm.

How long have you been working at Ernabella Arts?
I started working at Ernabella Arts in 1963. I grew up watching the women making rugs with wool when Ernabella Arts first started in 1948. Today I do the same kind of patterns on silk materials.

What sort of work do you do?
I work mainly with silk materials, scarves and occasionally T-shirts. I learnt to work with materials after going to Indonesia and seeing how it was done there. I have my own style now.

How has Ernabella Arts affected the community?
The community has always been very proud and supportive of the work that the women do at Ernabella Arts. The women from the communities meet regularly sharing ideas, learning together and going on trips to learn new things to do. This, I believe, is good for Ernabella Arts and the other art centres on the [Aboriginal] lands.

Do you train young girls there?
Yes, we do train young girls and even kids. They also have to learn about safety and the correct ways to use the equipment.

Is Ernabella Arts good for keeping the culture strong?
Yes. Firstly, we do keep our culture strong through our art; secondly, this is also a good way for our Tjukurpa to be documented and to make sure that the young people don't forget. We tell them Tjukurpa while we are painting.

From an interview between Nyukana Baker of Ernabella Arts and Lorna Wilson

TOP: DECKCHAIRS: (LEFT TO RIGHT) *NGURATJARA (VISIONS OF HOME)*, DESIGNED BY ERNABELLA ARTISTS, PRINTED BY MARIE WARREN; *KILIPI TJUTA (MANY STARS)*, DESIGNED BY NYUWARA TAPAYA, PRINTED BY MARIE WARREN; *MAKU (WITCHETTY GRUBS)*, DESIGNED BY VERA MBITJANA WILLIAMS, PRINTED BY MARIE WARREN.
BOTTOM: EDNA RUPERT CAREFULLY APPLIES A DESIGN IN WAX DIRECTLY ONTO SILK.

It's a good place; we work here all the time. It has had a big impact in our community. When it was new, and still now, people come in: young girls come and have a look, we teach them how to make pots.

We like the feeling of the clay — we can make it into anything: birds, animals, bushtucker, large murals. We have done other things — we always come back to clay. We make fun too, listen to music, have a little joke, make some small things just for fun. When we make money we use it for trips, to go and see how other people work. We have rules in here: no kids, no dogs. I make sure this place is kept clean. I [Judith] open it up in the morning and make sure the place runs well. We work all day and learn from each other, help each other, there's no competition. If someone does something new, we often have a go too. No one says mine is better than yours, everyone is happy for the other to do good work. We'd like to keep going for a long time.

Judith Inkamala and Carol Rontji

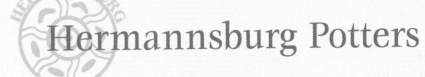

Hermannsburg Potters

JUDITH INKAMALA HANDBUILDS A POT WATCHED BY NAOMI SHARP, HERMANNSBURG POTTERS' TRAINER.

OPPOSITE PAGE: PARROTS SCREECH AND JOSTLE IN THIS VIBRANT MURAL, *ULBATJA (PORT LINCOLN PARROTS),* BY VERA WILLIAMS AND CAROL RONTJI.

Pottery was first introduced to Hermannsburg in the 1960s by missionaries working with the men of the community, but it was a series of training workshops in late 1990 on the outstations surrounding the town that has led to the establishment of the present thriving pottery studio which has an international reputation.

Hermannsburg, 130 km west of Alice Springs and home to 800 Western Arrernte people, was founded last century by Lutheran missionaries. The town first came to the world's attention in the 1930s through the delicately rendered watercolours of Aboriginal painter Albert Namatjira whose work led to what is now called the Hermannsburg school of watercolour artists. Many of the Hermannsburg Potters are descendents of these painters and grew up watching their relatives work. The potters have followed the tradition of artistic production but use the medium of clay to translate their cultural and artistic heritage.

With help from their pottery trainer, a practising ceramicist and teacher, and Denis Ebartaringa, a traditional custodian for the area, a small group of women, including established artists such as Judith Inkamala, Elaine Namatjira, Carol Rontji, Noreen Hudson, Esther Kennedy, Rahel Ungwanaka and Irene Entata, produce unique ceramic art in a small pottery studio in the centre of the community. Using a simple coil method, their readily identifiable style features small figures of birds, animals, lizards or plants which are sculpted onto the lids of the pots. Decoration, which narrates the stories of the figures, continues across the surface of the pot and

completes the story. The potters do not limit themselves to traditional images, however, and often incorporate fish, dragons, sharks and animals such as goats and zebras into their work. There is a preference for brightly coloured ceramic underglazes in landscapes painted on the pots of artists such as Elaine Namatjira, Judith Inkamala and Rahel Ungwanaka.

Frequently nowadays, the potters are engaged in the production of large, relief, clay tiles for murals. The brightly coloured murals feature landscape, wildflowers and birds from the local country and from the artists' Dreaming stories. The murals can be seen at interpretive displays and visitors' areas of national parks and tourist destinations around Alice Springs, including the Alice Springs Desert Park, and, elsewhere, at Taronga Park Zoo in Sydney, the Beverley Hills Library in California and many museums throughout Australia.

The freshness of a ceramic style which is not predictable is a compelling factor in the success of

TOP: SHELVES LOADED WITH HERMANNSBURG POTS READY FOR THE KILN.

BOTTOM: POT BY CAROL RONTJI.

the Hermannsburg Potters. The form of their work is generally not directed by a changeable art market. Their work is desirable because it combines originality and beauty: each piece is unique.

The Hermannsburg Potters have exhibited in major galleries around Australia and overseas. In 1992 five artists attended the Sixth South Pacific Festival of the Arts in the Cook Islands. In 1994 Maggie Watson, Hedwig Moketarinja and Noreen Hudson were invited to participate in a pottery and cultural exchange programme at the University of Santa Fe, USA with local Pueblo Indian potters and Ecuadorian potters. In 1996 Judith Inkamala, Maggie Watson, Esther Kennedy and Elaine Namatjira travelled to Lombok for an artists' exchange programme where they gave demonstrations of their craft to the indigenous Sasek potters of the island. Over the past few years their work has been exhibited in London, France, Italy, Holland, Taiwan and Singapore. Emerging artists of Hermannsburg include Vera Mbitjana Williams, Elizabeth Moketarinja, Clara Inkamala and Anita Ratara.

TOP LEFT: TILE SHOWING THE LOGO OF THE ALICE SPRINGS DESERT PARK.

TOP RIGHT: SMALL ANIMALS DECORATE THREE POTS BY JUDITH INKAMALA.

MIDDLE LEFT: CLARA INKAMALA AT WORK.

Ikuntji Women's Centre

I kuntji, also known as Haasts Bluff, is home to the Luritja people of the central Western Desert. It lies 230 km west of Alice Springs, nestled between two dramatic mountain ranges. The mountains that dominate the landscape around Haasts Bluff constitute important sites for the people of the area.

The Ikuntji Women's Centre at Haasts Bluff was opened in 1992. Acrylic painting on linen and handmade paper has earned the centre an impressive worldwide reputation. Today it has about 15–20 key artists who exhibit around Australia and overseas and their work is held in many public galleries and private collections.

The Ikuntji Women's Centre was initially set up to provide services such as catering for old people and children in the community and it still maintains this role, though over the years painting has dominated its operations. Bush trips organised by the Centre are important to the artists and their work. These trips are a source of inspiration for their paintings as well as an opportunity for artists to get back to their country, go hunting and affirm traditional links with the land.

To define the painting of the Ikuntji Women's Centre is difficult as the work created there is so diverse. Artists employ traditional symbols or inventive interpretations of their country and Tjukurrpa, or a combination of both. Artists such as Long Tom Tjapanangka and Narputta Nangala often paint on a large scale. Geometric patterning

and bold areas of colour are predominant in some work, particularly that of Mitjili Napurrula. Some artists employ a narrative approach, defining their country pictorially through images of plants, trees and flowers, as seen in the work of Daisy Napaltjarri Jugadai. However, uniting the work of the Ikuntji artists, and the work of emerging artists such as Alice Nampitjinpa, Eunice Napanangka and Linda Napurrula, is a stimulating use of colour and a strong sense of design. The artists are encouraged to produce bodies of work to be exhibited as solo shows, aimed at the contemporary, fine-art end of the art market. Several Ikuntji artists have secured arrangements with dealers in capital cities which ensures high exposure and increases the likelihood of acquisition by the major collections in Australia and overseas.

Securing regular ATSIC funding for the Centre has given the artists at Ikuntji a certain freedom to experiment. They paint and express their individuality with the latitude to develop as artists. The experimentation and innovation for which the painting from Ikuntji is known, has been received enthusiastically by collectors and galleries. The combination of a rich cultural heritage, which the artists draw upon for inspiration, and a highly developed sense of artistic freedom, has produced work that can stand alone in the international world of contemporary painting.

Everybody paints their Tjukurrpa here, I do my father's country – from Kintore.

Narputta Nangala

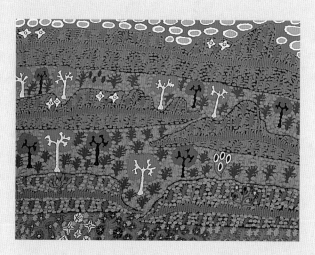

TOP: *UNTITLED* BY ALICE NAMPITJINPA, ACRYLIC ON LINEN, 116 cm x 88 cm.

BOTTOM: *IKUNTJI* BY DAISY NAPALTJARRI JUGADAI, ACRYLIC ON LINEN, 142 cm x 245 cm.

I started painting here in 1992, I learnt from school. I do a bit of painting and do a bit of teaching, when I finish school, learnt from here, this is better.

Everybody helps each other. We started on small canvas, did fabric and T-shirts and sewing, painted name [on the front of the Women's Centre], we eat good healthy food and clear up the kitchen.

We do painting only, and go to exhibitions everywhere. They likethis place, they want to do painting. Young girls have to do fabric and tie dyeing, women teaching young girls and do sewing.

This is my own country.

Daisy Napaltjarri Jugadai

TOP: HAASTS BLUFF.

MIDDLE: PAINTER NARPUTTA NANGALA WITH HER WORK *KARRKURUTINYTJA.*

BOTTOM: *WATYA TJUTA* BY MITJILI NAPURRULA, ACRYLIC ON LINEN, 137 cm x 153 cm.

Iwantja Arts and Crafts

Indulkana sits on what was originally a bare rocky ridge in the Everard Ranges in northern South Australia. The planting of hundreds of trees has transformed this bleak windswept face of the Great Victorian Desert as gums, casuarinas and flowering bushes emerge to hold the soil. The community is situated 50 km from Marla Bore, just off the Stuart Highway. The community and its homelands have a population of 400, mostly Yankunytjatjara, people who moved east from the Amata region many years ago.

When it first started the community's art and craft centre was called the 'Indulkana Arts Association'. Even though the centre's fortunes have fluctuated, it has always been home to many different artistic activities. In the early days people did patchwork, batik and *puṉu* (wood carving). Lino-block printing started in the early 1980s and became the medium through which Indulkana artists built their reputation nationally. The Family Centre building which houses the art and craft centre was damaged in January 1994 and was not rebuilt again for a nearly a year. During most of 1995 the re-emerging centre functioned without water or power — artists froze in the winter winds and sweltered in the summer. Regardless of the hardships, a new enthusiastic group of younger artists began producing work and Iwantja Arts and Crafts was formed.

Despite its rocky start, Iwantja artists have gained more and more experience as lino-block printers and the centre's reputation for printmaking continues to grow. Artists Vicki Cullinan and Julie Yatjitja display a strong sense of design and balance; colour is used adventurously and vigor-

TOP: VALERIE CULLINAN INKS A LINO BLOCK READY FOR PRINTING.

BOTTOM: *PUTIPULA*, A PRINT BY MARION BAKER.

ously, reflecting the mottled expanse of the surrounding country, the harsh bleakness of the desert, the proliferation of growth after rain. Tjinkuma Mingkili uses imagery in her prints based on traditional Dreaming stories and the collecting of bushtucker: a contemporary medium skilfully adapted to suit an indigenous content.

Artists from Iwantja Arts and Crafts have been involved in several important and highly successful workshops run by visiting artists from Alice Springs and Studio One in Canberra. This has resulted in the work of three artists — Valerie Cullinan, Marion Baker and Yilpi Ulah — being represented by two images in the 'Commemorative Print Folio Project for the Festival of the Dreaming' for the 2000 Olympics. Workshops have a major impact on techniques practised in the centre and experienced artists actively pass on skills to younger artists such as Joseanne Braedon and Kyra Bannington.

Recently Iwantja has begun to diversify their printmaking repertoire. Artists Mona Whiskey and Susie Prince (Presley) have produced one-off 2–3 m screen-printed fabric lengths and are also producing cards, stationery and a range of postcards. Other artists, such as Beverly Brumby and Jennifer Stewart, are painters working in a Western Desert style on canvas.

Iwantja Arts and Crafts is still a young art and craft centre constantly evolving and maturing, building a body of work. They sell and exhibit locally at Marla Bore and Coober Pedy and have been involved in exhibitions at the Adelaide Fringe Festival and the Araluen Centre in Alice Springs. They have shown work through World Visions, and have had art displayed in several regional galleries in South Australia.

TOP: IWANTJA FABRIC, SCREEN-PRINTED IN A VARIETY OF COLOURS.

BOTTOM: AN UNTITLED PRINT BY VALERIE CULLINAN.

JULIE YATJITJA CARVES A LINO BLOCK.

I have been working here for about one year. We learnt to do lino-block printing with trainers from Alice Springs and Studio One [printmaking studio] in Canberra. There are about ten of us who work here. It's a good place; I like doing training and workshops because it's good to learn new things. It's good for other people to come and learn and the community is proud; they like to see us doing things and selling things. People come in and buy things from us, we have secondhand clothes for the community, from Port Pirie, we sew curtains for our houses and aprons and clothes. We like to do T-shirts and the others wear them.

I am the Anangu [Aboriginal] coordinator and trainer. I help run the books, pay people for paintings and do time sheets. We have staff meetings where we talk about budgets and the things that we do in the centre. We'd like to do more lino-block printing and screen-printing and have exhibitions.

Valerie Cullinan

NGAPA (WATER) BY NAMPIJINPA DANIELS, 71 cm x 124 cm.

Jukurrpa Artists Corporation

JUKURRPA ARTIST BESSIE LIDDLE WORKING ON A PAINTING.

I n 1986 four women who were studying literacy at the Institute for Aboriginal Development (IAD) in Alice Springs started painting in the afternoons after classes. The activity caught on and, led by artists such as Bessie Liddle, Rachel Jurra, Maudie Nelson, Irene Boko and Kitty Miller, has evolved into the Jukurrpa Artists' Corporation with its own impressive studio and gallery located in the heart of Alice Springs. Today the Corporation represents the work of up to 600 people from across the Northern Territory, Western Australia and South Australia with a core group of artists managing the studio and gallery alongside an art coordinator.

'Jukurrpa' is the Dreaming or creation law of Aboriginal culture. It is a powerful word in many Central Australian Aboriginal languages and has meaning for all the 10 groups of Central Australia represented by the Jukurrpa Artists' Corporation: these include Warlpiri, Luritja, Anmatyerr, Arrernte, Pintupi, Yankunytjatjara, Ngaanyatjarra and Pitjantjatjara people. All the artists are drawn together by a shared respect for the Jukurrpa and a desire to use contemporary media to depict their Dreaming stories and chosen imagery.

Jukurrpa's artists are known for their experimentation, and their paintings, wooden artefacts and hand-painted jewellery are vivid and varied. A common thread through much of Jukurrpa's work is the use of colourful and intricate designs

We were studying at IAD [Institute for Aboriginal Development in Alice Springs] and painting after lunch. Then we had an idea: we wanted to start up our own gallery. We moved to a place on Gap Road but we were poor there, a few old canvases, a few of us were hanging on. So we made a few dollars by selling them and got some money from ATSIC and moved here [Stott Terrace]. We've been selling our canvases now. The Pitjantjatjara ladies are doing some necklaces as well, but only when we feel like it, mostly painting now. Tourists come and talk to us, ask us questions, what it's all about. We tell them the stories for the paintings, they come and sit with us. We show them how to mix colours, how to paint. We might tell them how we live, how we go for bushtucker, even how to speak language if they sit down with us for a little while.

We go into schools and teach culture, painting, dancing. School holidays we teach the little kids to do painting, how to dig for goanna and honeyants. Last year we went out to the Telegraph Station, we took all the young girls. All the girls and teachers got painted up for dancing. It's going well now!

Maudie Napanangka Nelson and
Rachel Napaljarri Jurra

TOP: *PUKA* BY KITTY MILLER, 61 cm x 126 cm.
MIDDLE: RACHEL JURRA WITH HER PAINTING *MALU (KANGAROO)* IN THE TODD RIVER AT ALICE SPRINGS.
BOTTOM: TOURISTS LOOK THROUGH PAINTINGS IN JUKURRPA'S GALLERY.

with subtle details reflecting the characteristics of the land, plants and animals from the Dreaming.

Alice Springs is a focal point for many Aboriginal people across Central Australia. When in town, visiting Aboriginal artists often work with Jukurrpa's painters in an outdoor work area next to the Corporation's gallery on Stott Terrace. Such contact has enabled Jukurrpa's members based in town to keep abreast of what is being produced in the bush and exposes them to other artistic styles and techniques. Being centrally located in Alice Springs has also given the artists frequent contact with tourists visiting town. They actively encourage tourists to come in and participate, talking about their work and explaining the stories rendered on their canvases. Jukurrpa artists are also actively involved with local school children and have given workshops and demonstrations at public events around Alice Springs.

The original core group of Jukurrpa artists has been joined by others including Alice Scobie, Bertha Dickson, Clarice Adamson, Christine Brown, Doris Egan, Marlene Boko, Kanakiya, Kim Butler, Janie Brown, Jodie Napangardi, Emily Rankin, Linda Syddick, and Margaret-Mary Turner-Neale. Their paintings and craft are often found in Jukurrpa's gallery. Some works are sent interstate to galleries in Cairns, Adelaide, Brisbane and Canberra. Since 1989 the organisation has been represented overseas in major exhibitions in London, New York, Santa Fe and Venice.

Looking to the future, Jukurrpa Artists Corporation is seeking to develop its skills in production and marketing, and are developing licensing agreements for a new range of products; they are also extending their studio area and gallery space.

WOMEN'S CEREMONIAL BODY PAINTING BY BESSIE LIDDLE, 82 cm x 130 cm.

Julalikari Council
CDEP Women's Art and Craft Programme

Wide grassy plains and lonely groupings of distinctive conical hills surround the town of Tennant Creek, which sits astride the Stuart Highway, 500 km north of Alice Springs. This is the Barkly region of the Northern Territory and the traditional home of the Warumungu people, many of whom make up the 3500 people who live in the town.

The Women's Art and Craft Programme, run through the Julalikari Council in Tennant Creek, had humble beginnings. It was set up in 1994 under the CDEP (Community Development Employment Programme) to meet the needs of local women who wanted to develop their skills in art production. At first they worked out of a tin shed with few resources and under difficult physical conditions. Then, in early 1995, they moved from the shed into a disused house in Mulga Camp (one of 10 urban Aboriginal living areas in the town).

The Pink Palace, as it is known locally, was originally a hostel for Aboriginal stockmen coming into town from out bush. The building had many uses before being renovated and decorated with blue and dusty pink murals to become an art and craft centre. It is now a meeting and workplace for women from the area, a thriving vibrant facility for a group of artists serious about their work. Much of their recent success can be attributed to the backing that the programme receives from Julalikari Council itself. The Council has helped fund new initiatives for the programme and has provided financial backing for artists to attend exhibitions and workshops. CDEP senior supervisors Nikkie Nangala Morrison and Jessica

OPPOSITE PAGE: *SOAKAGE* **BY PEGGY NAPANGARDI JONES, ACRYLIC ON CANVAS, 102 cm x 130 cm.**

Nangala Jones have assisted with the art and craft activities in addition to their duties as supervisors.

A variety of artwork is created by women at the Pink Palace: paintings, prints, ceramics and sewn garments. Through a training course run by Batchelor College, artists receive exposure to new techniques and media. They began recently, for example, to block print with lino and have enthusiastically embraced silk painting on scarves. The women have also gained a healthy reputation for hand-painted and hand-printed textiles. The fabrics produced have bright clear-cut designs, colours are vigorous and bold and they are distinctive amongst Central Australian textiles.

Julalikari Council Women's CDEP Art and Craft Programme is a relatively young art centre but it is rapidly becoming a recognised artistic force in the Barkly region. Artists have been involved in exhibitions in Tennant Creek and at the Araluen Centre in Alice Springs. Two artists from the centre recently held a very successful exhibition of hand-painted scarves at the historic Tennant Creek Telegraph Station; the show then toured to the AGOG Gallery in Canberra and to the Araluen Centre in Alice Springs. The Women's Art and Craft Programme has an annual end-of-year exhibition in Tennant Creek which has developed a dedicated following amongst the locals of the town.

Artists who work through the programme at Julalikari include: Michelle Napurrurla Frank, Peggy Napangardi Jones, Josephine Napangardi Grant, Kerry Napanangka Waistcoat, Leanne Napaljarri Chungaloo, Marlene Nakamarra Johnson, Elizabeth Nakamarra Johnson, Linda Nakamarra Dixon, Wendy Napurrurla Frank, Nikkie Nangala Morrison, Jessica Nangala Jones, Josie Nampijinpa Thompson, Doreen Napangardi Grant, Marlene Napanangka Rankine, Anna Nungarrayi Weston and Shirley Napangardi Plummer.

CDEP [Community Development Employment Programme] started in 1994 and I started here two years ago. I'm senior supervisor for those girls there, tell them what to do. It's a good job; I do painting and lino-block printing. When we first started we did murals — actually we do the same thing now, also painting and screen-printing — I like doing screen-printing now. It's a good job: nice workshop, nice people, things to do. We go on bush trips, some of the girls want to do these things, go out on bush trips with the old ladies, back to country.

Some of the ladies went on a trip to different art centres. We came back to Tennant [Creek] to do some of the things that we looked at. This gave us more strength to [try] different things. It's more friendly here. When we came in, we learnt landscape gardening. Now people have learnt to do new things, gives those ladies something to do. We have meetings every month, but not everyone, just us as bosses with the main office; we tell them what we want to do and what we'll do next. I've been working there since 1994 in the same job. I want to stay on here doing this.

Nikkie Nangala Morrison

DESERT COLOURS SWIRL AROUND BUSHTUCKER IMAGES IN A SILK SCARF BY PEGGY NAPANGARDI JONES, 90 cm x 90 cm.

ABOVE: SMALL JULALIKARI PAINTINGS ON DISPLAY IN THE
JULALIKARI STUDIO.

LEFT: SCREEN-PRINTED COTTON FABRIC BY (FROM LEFT TO RIGHT)
LINDA NAKAMARRA DIXON, PEGGY NAPANGARDI JONES AND
EUNICE WOODS.

BELOW: A BOLD FRESH DESIGN ON A SILK SQUARE BY PEGGY
NAPANGARDI JONES, 90 cm x 90 cm.

LIQUID SILK LENGHTHS BY (LEFT TO RIGHT) ANGKUNA TJITAYI,
INAWINYTJI WILLAMSON AND JUDY DAVIS.

Kaltjiti Arts and Crafts

TOP: ARTISTS WORK ON VARIOUS BATIKS IN THE KALTJITI ART AND CRAFT CENTRE; LEFT TO RIGHT: INAWINYTJI WILLIAMSON, POLLYANA SMITH, JUDY DAVIS AND KANGINY GEORGE.

BOTTOM: *MAI (BUSHTUCKER)* BY MARGARET WELLS, ACRYLIC ON CANVAS, 90 cm x 92 cm.

The country around the community of Fregon, at the foot of the Musgrave Ranges in the far north of South Australia, is expanses of sweeping sandy plains cut by winding creeks and punctuated by rocky outcrops. After rain these plains and the surrounding countryside come alive with colour. The community of Fregon is well known for its batik fabric which reflects these colours: warm pinks, yellows, vermilions, ochres and olive greens created with the Naphthol dyes which Fregon fabric artists use. The cloth is dipped and painted with these hues to form strong textural designs, echoing the pattern of the grassy plains.

The community of Fregon was established in 1961 as an outstation of Ernabella, 65 km to the north. It is located on the Pitjantjatjara Freehold Title Lands and has a population of 300 Anangu (Pitjantjatjara people).

In the early 1970s the Pitjantjatjara women of Fregon began producing art using the skills they had learnt at the nearby Ernabella mission. Ernabella Arts had been assisting women at Fregon for 10 years, helping them to develop skills in rug making, wool spinning, and wood carving. By 1975 the two organisations separated. The art centre at Fregon became known, firstly, as Aparawatatja Arts and Crafts and, later, became Kaltjiti Arts and Crafts.

In the early days, along with the techniques acquired at Ernabella, artists at Fregon sewed and produced tie-dyed fabric. Then the artists began painting onto small boards and working in batik.

The Kaltjiti art and craft centre has grown and now about 24 artists work there making

My name is Inawinytji Williamson and I have been working at Fregon since 1973 – 24 years. I have learnt to do paintings, make floor rugs, do batik – I like to work here and learn. Currently I am learning to do screen-printing onto fabric. Lots of people come to our centre to buy T-shirts, scarves, cards, canvas, artefacts such as little birds, boomerangs, necklaces, lizards and bowls.

There are many women who work in the craft room and some young girls come in too. They are learning. I am *Anangu Mayatja* of the Fregon craft room. I am also the chairperson and attend meetings there.

Inawinytji Williamson

TOP: INAWINYTJI WILLIAMSON AND DEBRA CURLEY DISPLAY
BATIK LENGTHS OUTSIDE THE KALTJITI ART AND CRAFT CENTRE.
BOTTOM: *UNTITLED* BY MARGARET WELLS AND YANYI WELLS,
ACRYLIC ON BOARD, 72 cm x 42 cm.

paintings, jewellery, batik and screen-printed fabric lengths. Their work is distinguished by the unmistakable flowing designs of the Pitjantjatjara artists of the region.

Unique watercolour paintings on board display an intricate patterning drawn from the natural environment and from the *walka* or artwork of the Pitjantjatjara people: the symbols created by the practice of *milpatjunanyi* (telling stories in the sand), and the designs that are painted on the body for various ceremonies. These watercolour paintings have evolved from the pastel drawings of schoolchildren into highly decorative works on quality paper. Artists mix the watercolour paint thickly to achieve the look of acrylic paint, shaping the medium into decorative swirls and spirals. The paintings comprise a central image in the framed space of the board: a self-contained motif within a defined border.

Batik was introduced in the early seventies and has become the technique most successfully practised at Fregon. Artists are now making iridescently coloured lengths of silk and cotton. These textiles, with their abstract arrangement of images edged by a detailed border design, are often up to 3 m in length and can take a week to complete.

Kaltjiti artists have recently begun working on hand-painted silk pieces. As scarves or as

framed works, the fabrics feature soft highlights in violets and blues mixed with gold gutta outlines. These pieces show an interesting transition in style from the larger batik lengths to smaller scale works.

Kaltjiti Arts and Crafts has participated in many exhibitions including the Indigenart Gallery Exhibition in Singapore, Italy and France; in the 1996 Adelaide Fringe Festival; and in the annual Central Australian Aboriginal Art Exhibition at Araluen. They have held three solo exhibitions in Adelaide and Perth. More recently, artists from the centre held their fourth solo exhibition at the Winkiku Centre at Uluru. This highly successful exhibition displayed a developing maturity and inventiveness and marked an important step in the evolution of Kaltjiti Arts and Crafts.

Artists who work at Kaltjiti include: Inawinytji Williamson, Mantuwa Treacle, Nyukana Norris, Margaret Wells, Yanyi Wells, Katie Curley, Tjunkaya Smith, Angkuna Tjitayi and Judy Davis.

BOLD PATTERNED SCREEN-PRINTED KALTJITI FABRICS FOLDED AND READY FOR SALE.

ABOVE: KERINGKE ARTEFACTS DISPLAY THE RICH INTRICATE
PATTERNING OF KERINGKE DECORATED OBJECTS.
RIGHT: KERINGKE ARTISTS.

OPPOSITE PAGE: LTYENTYE APURTE COMMUNITY

Keringke Arts

An intrigue with the new and different, combined with a love of painting on a variety of surfaces has brought constant change and development to the artwork of the people of Ltyentye Apurte community.

Ltyentye Apurte, or Santa Teresa, lies 80 km south-east of Alice Springs at the foot of a range of tabletop hills overlooking a sweeping plain. Situated between two large rocks, *Atyenhenge Atherre* (grandfather and grandson), Ltyentye Apurte was a sacred site before being established as a Catholic mission in the early 1950s. Under traditional law people were required to follow particular tracks across this country and to avoid certain areas. In 1976 the mission handed the land back to its traditional owners; today it is home to approximately 500 Eastern Arrernte people.

Art was part of the mission's schooling programme from the late 1950s. Local artists initially adopted a style similar to that of the Hermannsburg watercolour school of painting, interpreting their country in a style reminiscent of European representational art. Since the establishment of Keringke Arts, however, the imagery in their work has grown more symbolic — the connection to their indigenous heritage gradually growing stronger.

To the present day, all artists at Keringke Arts have been women; since 1987, more than 50 women have worked through the centre maintaining and expressing their culture through their art. The first Keringke Arts coordinator came to Ltyentye Apurte in 1987 to conduct a 15-week fabric painting course in the art room of the community school. This sparked much interest and demand for an arts-based enterprise in the community and today Keringke Arts operates from a purpose-built centre established in 1989. Agnes Abbott, Bridgette Wallace, Gabriella Wallace, Mary Oliver and, in particular, Kathleen Wallace, have been instrumental in establishing Keringke Arts as an internationally-renowned arts

PHOTO: STEVE STRIKE

organisation which produces distinctive colourful designs with an accomplished technique. Younger and newer artists, such as Camilla Young, Marie Young, Serena Hayes and Sharon Williams, continue to strengthen this reputation.

Historically, Keringke's reputation relates to works of art on silk. The luminous qualities of the fabric with the saturated rich colours of silk dyes produce the intricate and highly decorative creations that Keringke Arts is famous for. Delicate outlines in gold, copper or white express the personal style of each artist. The designs are filled with iridescent dyes such as vermilion, turquoise, aqua, gold and purple before finally becoming scarves, fine art lengths or items of wearable art.

Increasingly, Keringke artists have begun to translate their designs on to paper. This very successful transition has changed a previous recognition of Keringke work as fine craft work to its present status as fine art. They have further strengthened their profile as skilled and versatile artists through the production of decorative homewares: the surfaces of tables, chairs, boxes, mirror frames and ceramic pots are adorned with their signature

RIGHT: DETAIL OF A
SILK, *IRRERNTE-ARENYE
SINGING*, BY KATHLEEN
WALLACE (NATIONAL
GALLERY OF VICTORIA
COLLECTION).

OPPOSITE PAGE, TOP
RIGHT: DECORATED
BOXES ECHO THE PAT-
TERNS OF THE LTYENTYE
APURTE LANDSCAPE.
BELOW: UNTITLED WORK
BY CAMILLA YOUNG,
ACRYLIC ON PAPER
(ARALUEN CENTRE COL-
LECTION, ALICE SPRINGS).

style. These are popular items in galleries and good quality gift shops around Australia.

The majority of Keringke artworks are not accompanied by specific stories, yet artists do draw on a strong traditional narrative for inspiration, structured around age-old motifs, landscape forms, the elements, daily life, food gathering and the flora and fauna of the local countryside. Some artists, such as Jane Oliver and Mary Oliver, use a strong geometric style. However, all Keringke artists, including younger women like Jane and Bernadette Wallace, interpret this imagery to produce works that are both vigorous and innovative. Regardless of medium, professionalism and a rigorous attention to detail is standard practice at Keringke Arts.

Keringke artists were the first Aboriginal people to exhibit in the annual National Australian Craft Show, held in Sydney, in 1988. In the years since then Keringke Arts has participated in group exhibitions throughout Australia. In 1992 they toured New Zealand to meet with Maori artists and presented a solo exhibition at the Te Taumata Gallery in Auckland. While there they worked with local artists in a cultural exchange programme. Bridgette Wallace was awarded first prize in the Blundstone Boot Exhibition which toured Australia in 1993.

Artists from Keringke have also executed numerous commissioned projects. In 1997 Marie Young was commissioned to prepare designs for contemporary rugs and Jane Oliver has had works reproduced in a calendar featuring work from indigenous artists throughout Australia.

On-site training is especially important at the centre. Artists regularly work alongside visiting artists and teachers to receive exposure to new skills and media. Through these experiences, the visual language and skill base of the artists at Keringke continues to thrive. As they develop and mature, they continue to look to new media for artistic expression, expanding their product range and working towards economic independence.

Keringke Arts' centre was built for the women to do their painting, so they can teach their young ones the Dreamings and their culture. They all have different Dreamings and the elders teach them. The young ones can watch their elders and learn from them through paintings.

Kathleen Wallace

TOPSY TJULYATA AND WALTER PUKITIWARA WITH MARUKU WORK.

OPPOSITE PAGE: *KULATA* (SPEARS) READY FOR SALE AND DISTRIBUTION IN MARUKU'S WAREHOUSE.

Maruku Arts and Crafts

In 1981 a convoy of cars made a historic 300 km journey from the community of Amata east to Uluru. In the cars were Anangu (the Aboriginal people of the Central and Western deserts) artists, their families and two art coordinators, and they brought with them art and craft to sell. Together they set up a huge tent at the base of the tourist climb at Uluru. This became known as the *punu* tent and in two weeks this group sold more artwork than they could have sold in a whole year at Amata.

Word of the success of the expedition spread and soon many other communities in the Pitjantjatjara Lands joined the artists from Amata. This was the beginning of Maruku Arts and Crafts and in 1984 the organisation was officially formed. Among the original group of artists were Topsy Tjulyata, Walter Pukutiwara, Tony Tjamiwa and Pulya, who still remain the backbone of Maruku.

Maruku Arts and Crafts has become one of Australia's most successful Aboriginal craft co-operatives. Maruku is the trading arm of Anangu Uwankaraku Punu Aboriginal Corporation, meaning 'wood craft belonging to Anangu'. Today Maruku supports around 800 artists from more than 19 communities. It covers a vast area that crosses the Northern Territory, Western Australia and South Australia. It includes communities to the east of Uluru including Finke, Indulkana, Amata and Ernabella, right through to the west to Warburton, Warakurna, Tjukurla, Pipalyatjara and Docker River. These communities are visited every six weeks by the *punu* truck, craft is purchased, tools supplied and discussions on market trends take place.

I've been making a lot of small lizards, thinking about and learning to carve all sorts of different things. I was beginning to make them really well and to think about selling them. And when they said to me, 'Hey, who made those things and gave them to you?' I replied that I'd taught myself . . . And I carved and carved and carved a lot to sell, trying hard to do it well, making the *punu* [wood craft], making this craft. I made birds as well and then we came to Uluru with our *punu*, bringing it to where people climb the rock, selling it in the beginning from the base of the climb. We sat down there with a lot of our *punu*, making it, learning to sell it to the tourists. We've been selling and selling, learning all the time and now we have our Cultural Centre to display our work in.

We've been working really well for a long time now, going to the creekbeds, collecting wood to carve, bringing it back to make many many things.

Pulya Taylor

A long time ago I was living in Amata and one of the white people there asked us if we'd make some *punu* [wood craft]. So we thought about what we would make and began the carving. At first it was really rough work − we were trying but weren't very skilful, but from those days we've learnt a lot.

We were thinking and thinking, always thinking as we were carving, and learning, and I decided to make a carving like a *ngintaka* [perentie lizard], making its feet and hands, carving its head and a long tail and it turned out really well. I then used wire to burn the *walka* [design] on it, we were just learning this skill. Later we used it to decorate *wira* − small bowls − just like our grandmothers had made in the past.

After this we began to talk about how best to make the craft and to take it to places where we could sell it. And we've taken it to exhibitions where many people have bought a lot of *punu*, which is really wonderful.

We then came to Uluṟu with Pat and Peter, bringing a great load of *punu*, all of it on the truck to sell to the tourists. We've come to understand a lot about this business, sending *punu* out to other places, other people coming to buy it from here. People have come to really want our *punu*, we've been making it so well. We've been learning and practising this craft for a long time now and we've become very experienced.

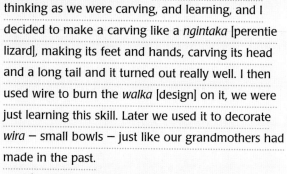

TOP: SNAKES BY BILLY COOLEY.

MIDDLE: SPEARS, DIGGING STICKS AND COOLAMONS SIT ON THE SAND-DUNES OF ULUṞU.

BOTTOM: *KULATA* (SPEARS).

Topsy Tjulyata

From bough shelters at the old *punu ngura* (wood-craft place), Maruku moved in 1995 to its expansive gallery in the new Uluru–Kata Tjuta Cultural Centre near the base of Uluru. A wide range of art, predominantly carved and decorated wooden artefacts and traditional weapons, is available there. The range of smaller souvenirs includes animals, *ininti* (bean tree) bead jewellery and coolamons. Large and unusual fine art and craft pieces such as large and twisted snakes and lizards made from tree roots are also produced and many of these are purchased by museums and private collections. Maruku operates an extensive warehouse in the Mutitjulu community, from where works are sent across Australia and throughout the world.

Anangu are proud of Maruku and they are proud of what is sold through the organisation, providing them as it does with the means to represent their culture appropriately. Functional objects are still made today as they were made by ancestors in the Tjukurpa, the traditional system of law that governs people's lives. The barb of a *miru* or spearthrower is still tied with kangaroo sinew and the stone blade in its handle fixed with *kiti* or spinifex resin. There are also unique animal carvings and more contemporary objects produced which still display the strong connection that artists have to their country.

Artists represented by Maruku have works in many prestigious collections including the National Gallery of Australia, Queensland Art Gallery, Museum of Victoria, Australian National Museum, Araluen Art Centre, the Kelton Foundation, USA and the Osaka Museum in Japan.

CARVED WOODEN ANIMALS ON A DESERT SAND-DUNE.

TJUNGINPA **BY MICK NAMARARI TJAPALJARRI, ACRYLIC ON LINEN, 122 cm x 122 cm.**

Papunya Tula Artists Pty Ltd

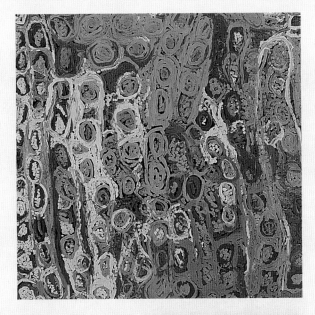

QUOLL DREAMING **BY
MAKINTI NAPANANGKA,
ACRYLIC ON LINEN,
122 cm x 122 cm.**

Papunya Tula Artists Pty Ltd is recognised as being the longest running community-based art company in Central Australia. Incorporated in 1972, this wholly Aboriginal owned and directed company represents 200 artists and craftspeople, mainly from the Pintupi and Luritja language groups. These artists are spread across four major communities — Kintore, Kiwirrkura, Mt Liebig and Papunya — in a region that extends over 720 km west from Alice Springs. The focus of the company in its early days, however, was Papunya, an Aboriginal settlement 240 km north-west of Alice Springs. Papunya Tula Artists Pty Ltd is named after the community and one of the nearby hills known as Tula, a Honeyant Dreaming site.

Papunya settlement was established in the late 1960s by the government as a base for Aboriginal people from the surrounding areas who had been forcibly removed from their traditional lands. Today, many people have moved back to their homelands and continue a tradition of strong ceremonial ties to the country.

In 1971, with encouragement from a young school teacher, Mick Namarari Tjapaltjarri, Timmy Payungka Tjapangati, Yala Yala Gibbs Tjungurrayi and other men from Papunya began painting onto canvas and boards. They painted motifs drawn from the traditional ceremonial body and sandpainting associated with their Tjukurrpa — the law of the country and the Dreaming. This exciting progression heralded what is famously known as the Western Desert Art movement.

Papunya Tula Artists was set up in response

to the world's fascination with the new art form. It protects the artists' interests and assists in the maintenance of their culture. The company is controlled by a body of five directors, who are themselves artists. Within the broader hierarchy, an older group of key artists support the development of the younger up-and-coming artists while they gain experience as painters. There is a company-run gallery outlet in Alice Springs, but Papunya Tula Artists remains a community-based organisation with field workers spending over half their time in the participating communities.

The work of the Papunya Tula Artists is bold and sophisticated. From its early days of symbolism and organic imagery, the paintings today are characterised by intense line work with a strong geometric structure, executed in the simple earthy colours of the Central Desert. The company also sells craft items such as jewellery and carved wooden artefacts on behalf of artists. Artists working through Papunya Tula, such as Tula Ronnie Tjampitjinpa and Turkey Tolson Tjupurrula, have produced limited edition woodblock prints on paper.

In 1982 women from Mt Liebig and Papunya, in particular Eunice Napangardi and Pansy Napangardi, began working for the company. They often work on a large scale, creating paintings which feature the bushtucker of the country around Papunya. After a collaborative exhibition with women from the Ikuntji Women's Centre at Haasts Bluff, women from Kintore also began painting through Papunya Tula. The paintings of Tatali Nangala, Inyuwa Nampitjinpa and Nyurpaya Nampitjinpa are filled with spirited fluid forms on mottled and textured backgrounds. These women held their first successful exhibition as a group at Papunya Tula's gallery space in Alice Springs in 1996.

The high standard of its work and its unmistakable powerful style, has resulted in steady growth and development for the company. Exhibitions which have added to their reputation include the 1988 Brisbane Expo where 27 artists completed individual works 3–7 m long; and the critically acclaimed 'Dreamings' exhibition which toured though USA, Britain and Europe. Today, Papunya Tula Artists are represented in major museums, galleries and private collections worldwide and participate each year in more than 10 national and international exhibitions.

LEFT: *WOMEN'S DREAMING* BY TATALI NANGALA, ACRYLIC ON LINEN, 91 cm x 91 cm.

OPPOSITE PAGE, TOP: *SNAKE DREAMING* BY YALA YALA GIBBS TJUNGARRAYI, ACRYLIC ON LINEN, 152 cm x 122 cm.

BOTTOM LEFT: *TINGARI DREAMING* BY GEORGE TJUNGURRAYI, ACRYLIC ON LINEN, 122 cm x 122 cm.

BOTTOM RIGHT: THE PAPUNYA TULA GALLERY ON TODD STREET IN ALICE SPRINGS.

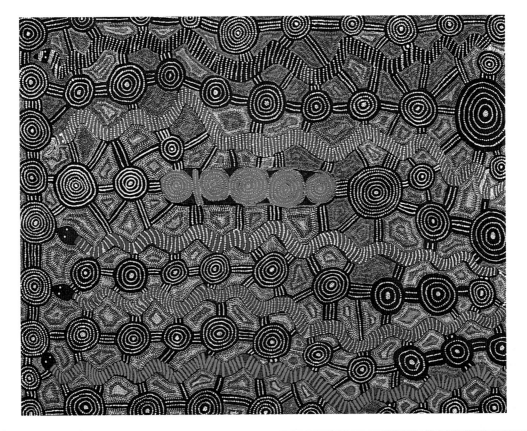

I've been working with Papunya Tula for 25 years, still working there. I'm working there now. I always do big pictures. I always paint with Papunya Tula. I paint my father's and grandfather's Dreaming. I was born north of Lake Mackay, I'm living at Ntarpa Camp now. Always sell through Papunya Tula, it's a good place. I've been going to Melbourne, for the Gabrielle Pizzi show with Michael Nelson Tjakamarra. Always painting, keeps me working.

Timmy Payungka Tjapangati

PRINTED AND HAND-PAINTED MATERIALS OF TITJIKALA.

Titjikala Women's Centre

J ust off the old South Road that follows the original Ghan railway track, about 100 km south of Alice Springs, lies the small community of Titjikala. Desert oaks and red sand-dunes punctuate the dusty journey to the community that was originally set up as a stock-camp for nearby Maryvale Station. About 180 people from predominantly Luritja and Pitjantjatjara language groups live here. Not far along the road is Chambers Pillar, a sheer molar-like column of heavy red rock that marked a significant point on the maps of the European explorers of the mid-19th century.

The Women's Centre at Titjikala has been in operation for eight years. Its fortunes have fluctuated over this time, however, because of changes in community staffing, artists coming and going, and some major difficulties with funding. Throughout all this, however, it has maintained its important industrious role in the community. Today, women such as Annie Wallace, Susan Amungara and June Wiluka run a catering and home-care programme for old people alongside the production of artwork. The community's pride in the Titjikala Women's Centre is demonstrated by the support it receives from the Titjikala Community Council. The Council supports and totally finances the Centre and acts in an advisory capacity.

The Centre is establishing itself as a working studio for artists to practise their craft and train in new areas. Artists Doris Thomas, Rene Douglas and Lena Campbell produce paintings in the Central Desert style, jewellery, batik and wood carvings. Their art is an interesting mix of the tra-

TITJIKALA ARTISTS AT WORK AT THE WOMEN'S CENTRE.

This place has been going for a few years now. We do paintings and screen-printing. We had a trainer come in and help us. I like to do dot paintings here and at home. Linda [the coordinator] takes them into the Todd Mall Sunday market.

There's a lot of young girls working here; there's nowhere else they can work at home. Older women come in, clean up, rake the yard, some help do the washing for the older people. They do meals on wheels for the pensioners here too.

People are proud of this place. Some of the old ladies take the young girls down to the creek and learn dance, bush corroboree and tell stories. It's a good way of keeping stories strong.

Lena Campbell

ABOVE: CARVED AND DECORATED WOODEN ANIMALS ON A SAND-DUNE NEAR TITJIKALA. RIGHT: RENE DOUGLAS WORKS ON A PAINTING.

ditional and contemporary. Images of the Dreaming trails that wind across the surrounding country are worked in delicate arrangements on the small canvases and boards of Josie Mulder and Lisa Wiluka. Others, like Mavis Wari and Dora Wari, produce carved wooden artefacts of small animals and lizards which are completed at home with their own familiar tools and fire. The repertoire of the Titjikala artists has broadened through recent workshops in screen-printing and silk painting.

The Titjikala Women's Centre has been in several local exhibitions in Alice Springs. They also regularly sell their work at markets and art fairs. In 1996 an evening gown made from a batik by Doris Thomas was presented at the Northern Territory Fashion Awards.

TOP: A DESERT BREEZE CATCHES DORIS THOMAS' SILK BATIK.

BELOW: HAND-PRINTED BAGS WITH DESIGNS THAT REFLECT THE

COLOUR AND SHAPE OF THE LOCAL LANDSCAPE.

Utopia Cultural Centre
and Awely Batik Corporation

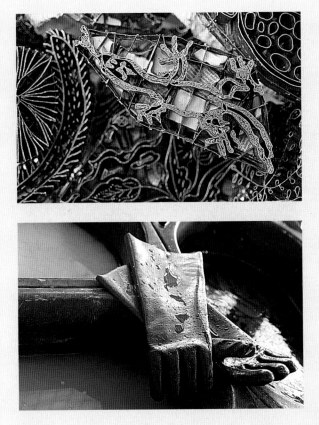

TOP: METAL TJAPS READY FOR APPLYING WAX DESIGNS ON FABRIC.

OPPOSITE PAGE: WIND AND SUN DRY A SILK BATIK LENGTH BY ROESE PWERL.

Utopia is located on the Angarapa Land Trust, which is spread over gently undulating and mostly arid country in the south-eastern region of the Northern Territory and to the north of Alice Springs. It is the homeland of about 800 Anmatyerr and Alyawarr people who in 1978 successfully reclaimed their traditional country which for the previous 50 years had been the Utopia Pastoral Lease. The Land Trust covers a vast area of some 2500 sq km, including 20 outstations and homelands, and is traversed by the Sandover Highway which winds dustily northwards towards the Queensland border. The surrounding scrubby woodland country is divided by sand ridges, rocky outcrops and wide sandy creekbeds that remain dry for much of the year. Ancestral Dreaming trails crisscross the homelands and the land is considered sacred country under Aboriginal law.

Batik has been synonymous with Utopia since the technique was introduced to the community in a training programme run by the Institute for Aboriginal Development in the late 1970s. Pitjantjatjara artists, skilled in the Ernabella method of batik making, shared the technique with the Utopia women and the rest is history!

Over the years these batiks have evolved into works of art on fabric characterised by a spontaneous fresh style. Strong ties to land and to women's *awely*, or ceremony, provide a rich spiritual and creative reserve for artists. The silks are a mosaic storyboard of camp life, of the gathering of bushtucker and of nurturing and maintaining clan and country.

Artists combine various methods of wax

application in the batiks. Wax can be painted directly on the fabric or worked with a *tjanting* tool or *tjap* printing block, a technique acquired during a cultural exchange to Indonesia in 1994. Prominent batik artists are Glory Angal, Mavis Akemarr, Nora Apetyarr and Roese Pwerl.

The Utopia Cultural Centre and Awely Batik Corporation promotes other art forms produced by the artists of the region. Painting in acrylic on canvas was first introduced to Utopia in the late 1980s and the artists took to the medium with the same instinctive directness and vivacity that is widely recognised as the Utopia style. Wooden sculptures of animal, bird and human forms, often painted in bold bands of colour, are made by both men and women. Wally Pwerl, Billy Morton, Katie Kngwarrey and Donny Young Angal are all renowned wood sculptors. Fine art prints of artists' works have been produced; key artists from the community involved in the print programme include Dave Ross Pwerl, Lindsay Bird Ampetyan, Greeny Purvis Apetyarr, Lena Pwerl and Ada and Gloria Apetyarr.

The Utopia Cultural Centre is regularly involved in training and workshops, demonstrating techniques at festivals and as accompaniment to exhibitions. The artists have given training classes to many Central Australian Aboriginal communities conducted at Hamilton Downs Youth Camp, and demonstrated various techniques at the Seventh Pacific Festival of the Arts in Samoa in 1996. During the 1997 Festival of the Dreaming, the first indigenous cultural event leading up to the Sydney Olympics, Utopia artists demonstrated their art making as part of a special exhibition at the Powerhouse Museum as guests of the Sydney Organising Committee for the Olympics Games. Over the 1997 to 1998 Christmas period, Utopia Awely Batik exhibited in Paris at the Parc De La Villette in a blockbuster show comprising 30 extraordinary 5 m-long batik silks. A group of artists including Gloria Apetyarr and Ada Bird Apetyarr attended the exhibition to complete a large commissioned sandpainting and conduct batik demonstrations to augment the show.

The art of Utopia continues to feature in numerous exhibitions around Australia and has been acquired into major public collections throughout the world.

TOP: MAVIS AKEMARR, SILK BATIK, 3m LENGTH.

Our *awely* [women's ceremony] is from my grandfather and grandmother on my father's side and my father. That's it. Kathleen Akemarr has been teaching me for a long time since I was a kid, I never lose it. I pass it on to my nieces and cousins. My grandaughter she knows.

This Alhalker and Atnangker Dreaming for country. This is Little Lizard, Thorny Devil Lizard, Emu, Dog and Long Thin Yam and Yam Flower Dreaming. Also Ntyerrm Dreaming — that's the dogwood seed.

Awely is real important. It is the Dreamtime when everything began. *Awely* dance and song makes people happy and strong when they are sick. With *awely* they get fat again. *Awely* holds up country. Women have the *awely*, not men. The body painting is *awely*, goes a long way from Utopia right up to Tennant Creek and all the way to Three Ways where it branches off somewhere — might be to Arnhem Land.

At Three Ways is Jurnkurakurr, a sacred water-hole. The people from long time back have been knowing it as a dangerous place. They will only drink the water if they first put leaves in the water-hole. The leaves make it all right. The body scars are made to heal sickness and they are *awely* also.

Awely is everything. *Awely* is the whole lot.

Gloria Tamerr Apetyarr

ABOVE: FABRIC IS DIPPED BY ROESE PWERL AGAIN AND AGAIN IN SUCCESSIVE DYE BATHS TO BUILD A RICH PATINA OF COLOUR.

BELOW: *BUSH ORANGE*, ETCHING AND ACQUATINT BY LENA PWERL, 17 cm x 20 cm.

BOTTOM: ADA BIRD APETYARR, SILK BATIK, 3m LENGTH.

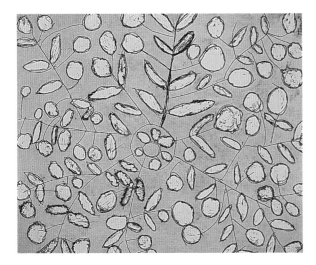

VIBRANT WALKATJARA GLASSWARE GLOWS IN THE DESERT LIGHT.

Walkatjara Art Centre

Mutitjulu community, located inside Uluru–Kata Tjuta National Park at the base of Uluru, is in the heart of the red sand-dune and spinifex country of the southern end of the Northern Territory. Two-hundred and twenty Anangu, or Pitjantjatjara and Yankunytjatjara people, live at the community.

A women's centre which was located at the 'straw house', one of the original houses on the community, initially provided an art studio area for the women of Mutitjulu. The straw house was so named as it was lined with straw for insulation against the searing temperatures of summer and the cold desert winter winds. The women's centre ran various art programmes which provided specialist tutors to work with local artists and allowed the artists to gain important contact with new skills and media.

HAND-PAINTED CERAMIC PLATES BY (LEFT) RENE KULITJA AND (RIGHT) PAMELA TAYLOR.

Recently, the women's centre art activities were incorporated with the activities of the Walkatjara Trust. Walkatjara (which means 'objects having designs') is a community enterprise which designs, manufactures and markets souvenir products. Today, the Walkatjara Art Centre operates from the straw house and is known for a range of products, particularly hand-painted ceramics and glassware.

Ceramic work began on the community in 1993 when Mutitjulu artists attending various classes at the straw house began developing skills in designing artwork for transferring onto ceram-

We create designs of Tjukurpa [Anangu law and religion] from our grandmothers' and grandfathers' country. They tell our fathers and mothers. And mothers and fathers in turn tell us the stories. And we listen and in turn tell our children. And the children listen and remember. And we are happy and content to know these stories.

Dora Taylor and Rene Kulitja

TOP: ARTISTS LISA LONG (LEFT) AND SUSAN BOURKE (RIGHT) PAINT CERAMIC PLATES READY FOR FIRING.
LEFT: GLASS RIDGES OF A SLUMPED, SANDBLASTED AND SCREEN-PRINTED PLATTER ECHO THE ULURU SAND-DUNES.

OPPOSITE PAGE, TOP: HAND-PAINTED CERAMIC PLATES BY (LEFT) KATIE LYONS AND (RIGHT) PAMELA TAYLOR. BELOW: BLOWN AND ENGRAVED WALKATJARA GLASSWARE.

ic surfaces. They learnt about the techniques of applying glazes to bisque ware and have gone on to produce a range of individually designed and hand-painted ceramics. A blend of traditional Western Desert designs and strong organic shapes distinguish their unique clear style. The added impact of a medium little employed by other Aboriginal people in Central Australia heightens the freshness of their work.

In 1994, through a training programme run at the community, women were introduced to the process of slump glass production. Since then, they have participated in glass workshops run by the University of South Australia and, more recently, in the Glass Workshop at the Canberra School of Art. The artists now use a broad range of glass production techniques including glass engraving, screen-printing on glass, painting with powdered glass and glass enamels, sandblasting and moulding. Their individual and highly origi-

nal works of art demonstrate an unmistakable artistic style and reflect a vibrant culture.

Recently Walkatjara Art Centre artists have started hand painting and screen-printing onto fabric. Some of the artists working through the Centre are Rene Kulitja, Katie Lyons, Jennifer Taylor, Pamela Taylor, Pirmangka Nipper, Patricia Patterson, Mauna Ailek, Roslyn Ailek, Dora Taylor and Rene Tiger. The Australian National Gallery recently purchased three engraved Walkatjara glass pieces.

KUNGKARANGKALPA TJUKURRPA AT WANARN (SEVEN SISTERS AT

WANARN) BY KANYTJURI BATES, DETAIL OF TWO GLASS PANELS,

EACH 20 cm x 11 cm.

Warburton Arts Project

In the red gravel and spinifex break-away country of the mid-eastern region of Western Australia, and not far from the Northern Territory border, is the community of Warburton. Over 500 people from the predominantly Ngaanyatjarra language group live in the community, which lies on one of the main routes between Western Australia and the Northern Territory.

In 1991 the Warburton Arts Project was begun with the brief of maintaining and strengthening the cultural life of the community. Through a series of art training programmes a substantial collection of artwork has been accumulated. These works constitute an important cultural and artistic development in the Warburton area and today the collection numbers over 250 works.

The emphasis of the Warburton Arts Project is cultural relevance. All activities occurring in the Project's centre are followed according to indigenous protocol. Arts practice is seen as part of a broader expression, part of a larger picture, which incorporates appropriate systems of documentation and curation. Men's and women's paintings are documented, recorded and housed in separate locations according to customary law. A substantial database, and video and audio tapes are used in the documentation of these paintings, recording such details as the artists' genealogies and family ties, stories and places. These vigorous works, which depict artists' ties and tenure to the land, are being used in evidence in native title claims.

The Warburton Glass Project is another facet of the Warburton Arts Project and has been in operation for two years. The Glass Project was ini-

PHOTO: GARY PROCTOR

THE ROAD TO WARBURTON.

I'm Tjingapa Davies and I live in Warburton since I was a very young girl. I used to live in the Warburton Home where I grew up. Our parents put us in the home. When I was living in the Home I worked, sweeping the floor and washing the dishes. The

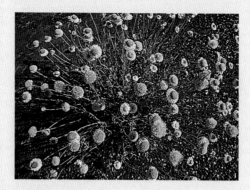

girls and boys slept in separate beds but all in the one room. Later on, they built a separate home for the boys and a woman called Mrs Mack cared for the boys. One of the things that I loved doing in the Home was making bread. Every evening we would prepare the mixture and place it into greased tins to allow the dough to rise overnight. In the morning we would get so excited when we saw the raised dough. Each morning we would bake the bread and have the bread for supper.

Now we are working with Albie and Karliwalyku. We cut the shapes [glass] and place them around the big bowl then we place the glass thing on top. We don't walk around much. We just stay in our workplace working on our bowls. At the end of the day we clean and sweep our workplace so it's nice and clean all the time. At work the next day we love admiring our dishes as we get them out of the oven as they look beautiful. When the dishes have cooled down we wash them in hot water, dry them and display them on the table for people to come and see.

My husband, my brother Cyril, and Elizabeth and myself used to go to the place Kalkakutjarra. My husband was born in Kalkakutjarra. Albie and Karliwalyku would take us to Kalkakutjarra. My husband, my brother and Karliwalyku would paint pictures in the cave there. At lunchtime they would come and have lunch and then head back to the cave to paint some more.

Another thing that Albie, Elizabeth and myself would do is go out to get honeyants. We would come back home with a cupful of honeyants. Another time we might go out to collect the bushtucker desert raisin. We also paint Tjukurpa stories on canvas and recount Tjukurpa stories and go out to the places that related to them. Albie, a woman from Sydney, and myself would go out to Lurtju, Mitika and Wanarn to paint the Tjukurpa pictures in the caves.

We took photos of the man in the Kungkarangkalpa Tjukurpa story. The man happened to hit his nose when he was on top of the mountain. At the time when the man hit his nose the Seven Sisters were close to him. The man didn't have a fire so he went down to get some wood when he hit his nose and died. Poor thing!

We also do work on our genealogies and Dorothy would take photos of us in our own country. We are doing much important and difficult work in the bush. We went to the site, the big hole, where the Warnampi [Water Snake] swallowed the two children, a boy and a girl. This episode is part of a Tjukurpa story. The father of the children couldn't find his children anywhere and realised that something terrible had happened to them, so, in his great sorrow, he began hitting himself on the head with a rock and rolled around on the ground crying for his children. Dorothy took a photo of us at the big hole where the Warnampi went into the ground.

Another thing that Elizabeth and I do is to prepare the pieces of canvas for the people to paint their own Tjukurpa stories on.

Tjingapa Davies (Transcribed and translated from Ngaanyatjarra by Lizzie Ellis)

tially set up as a community initiative to produce glass panels for the Warburton Civic and Cultural Centre. Glass production at Warburton is hands-on, artists are involved in the process at every stage, designing and producing large panels of glass up to 2 m long. The smooth face of these glass panels has given the artists a clean surface to adorn with individual iconography and images. The dynamic play of light against the etched designs of the glass produces works of great beauty and sophistication. Panels have been commissioned by major galleries and institutions around Australia. In early 1998 large glass panels together with a collection of glass platters were exhibited publicly for the first time as part of the Festival of Perth at the Fremantle Arts Centre.

The repertoire of the artists extends beyond just the architectural to domestic objects. Platters and bowls are afforded the complexity given to the larger panels. Examples are held in outlets around Australia, building the Warburton Art Project's reputation for glass production. Artglass, like the paintings of Warburton, is practised in the Project's centre as a means of cultural expression for Ngaanyatjarra people. The cultural relevance of the designs is complemented by the fresh qualities of a new medium resulting in works with a clear traditional content in a contemporary space.

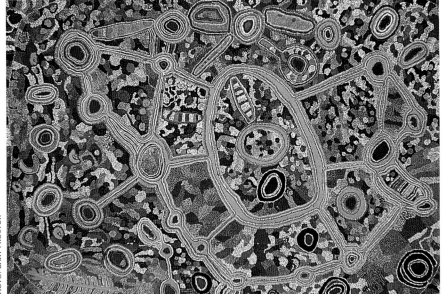

PHOTO: GARY PROCTOR

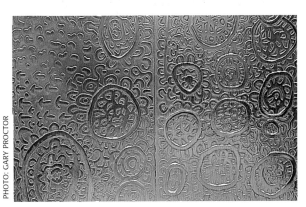

PHOTO: GARY PROCTOR

ABOVE: *WIRRIRRPI* **BY PULPURU DAVIES, ACRYLIC ON CANVAS.**

LEFT: *KUNGKARANGKALPA TJUKURRPA AT WANARN (SEVEN SISTERS AT WANARN)* **BY TAPARTI BATES, DETAIL OF TWO GLASS PANELS, EACH 20 cm x 11 cm.**

Yuwa! Ngankunyarna Elizabeth Holland-nga, walykunyarna watjalku ngayuku waarkatjarra ngankulurna Warburton-ta palyantjatjarra. Tirtulatju yankupayi Karlkakutjarra-kutu pulpangka walka palyaratjaku. Warburton-ta ngamu ngarrala Karlkakutjarra-nya. Yankupayilatju Albie-nya, Gary Proctor-nya, Mr and Mrs Davies-nga kamu Mr Holland-nga. Karlkakutjarra-latju tjarpara mungangka ngaripayi. Tjirntungkalatju pakarra yankula pulpakutu tjarpara walka paint-timalpayi, paint-timarralatju mungaripayi.

Walkalatju paint-timarra, ngayukulampa Tjukurpa pirnitjarra. Walka pirninyalatju palyarailku wiyaralpi marlaku Warburton-ku yankupayi. Warburton-talatju painting-pa palyara canvas-pangka, painting pirnilatju paint-timarra.

Kalala kutjungkalatju yanu Mitikaku. Mitikanya ngankuku kuriku ngura, Mitikalalatju tjarparalpi mirrka ngalangu wiyaringkula pulpakutu yanu. Pulpa purlkanya wiya, pulpa kulunypa. Nyinaralatju pulpangka paint-timaranytja. Cyril-tu, Mr Davies-tju kamu Karliwalykulu paint-timarranytja pulpangka. Wati ngaaluya watiku tjumatjarra walka pulpangka paint-timarranytja. Kalala rawalatju paint-timarra, tii kamu mirrka ngalkula kutjulatju paint-timarranytja. Mungaringu nyangkalatju ngurakutu yankulalpi mirrka ngalangu kunkunaringu. Ngaringulatju tjinturingkulalpi purrurtu yanu pulpakutu paint-timanu wiyarralpi marlaku Warburton-ku yanu.

Mitikalatju yanu pulpangka paint-timanu wiyaringu pitjangu Warburton-ta nyinangu partu artglass start-timaralpi palyarranytja. Albie-lulanyatju nintipungu artglass-pa palyaltjaku. Palunyalulanyatju board-pa yungkulalpi nintipungu katapungkula shapes-pa palyaltjaku. Nintiringulatju board-pa katapungkula, tarkarlmankula shapes-pa pirninya bowl-pangka para-tjunkulatjaku. Walykunyantalatju wiya walykumunu mularpa,

yungaralu artglass-pa palyarra. Artglass-palatju yungaralu pitjala every morning-pa palyarra nyangka Albie-lu waarka kutjupa pirni palyarra. Artglass plate-pa kamu bowl-palatju tirtu rawalu palyarra. Kumuniti pirningkalapatjuya Arnangulu kamu walypalalu payipungkulalpi kanyirra. Walykunyalatju minyma pirnilu special artglass-pa palyarra tjunkukitjalu Cultural Centre nyuwanpangka. Walypala pirniya mukuringkula ngankukulampatju artglass bowl-ku kamu plate-ku palunyatjanuluya watjarra artglass plate-pa kamu bowl-pa Warburton-nga martatji mantjilkitjalu.

Ngankunyarna kamu minyma kutjupa-tjarranyalatju tirtu pitjapayi Albie-ku ngurakutu, dot painting-pa nyinara palyarranyinakitjalu. Ngarnmanytjulatju kulilpayi Tjukurpa ngananyatjarra paint-timalkitjalu, tjukurpalatju ngurkarntalpi, Tjukurpa palunyanya canvas-pangka paint-timalpayi. Kalala kutjupangkalatju yankupayi Albie-lawana kamu staff member kutjupa-tjarralawana purtikutu. Purtingkalatju ngura tjunkula ngaripayi palunyalulatju yinkara Tjukurpa pakalpayi. Purtingkalatju flowers-pa pirni nyakupayi palunyalulatju tjananya walypala staff pirninya nintipungkupayi tjiinya ngari tjawaltjaku, tirnka kamu pinytjatarnpa tjawarra pungkutjaku. Kutjupalatju palyalpayi tjiinya purnulatju kartarra tjaalimarra walypalakutu.

Walykunyalatju tamalmarra palyarra tjunkula Cultural Centre nyuwanku. Mrs Davies-tju, Lala-lu kamu minyma kutjupa-tjarralulatju waarka kutjulpitulpi-ngurru tirtu waarkaringu. Waarkangkalatju nyinangu, nyinangu tirtu walykunya nyinara. Ngaangurrulatju tirtu palyanmalpa artglass plate-pa, bowl-pa kamu dishes pirni-nya.

Albie-lawanalulatju waarka walykumunu mularpa palyarra! Ngulayan nganku-kulampatju artglass work-pa nyakulalpi nintilu kuliiku munta Warburton minymaluya ngaanya palyarnu.

Palunyarna watjarnu wiyaringu.

Yes! I'm Elizabeth Holland and I'm going to tell you about myself and the work that I do, and have done, in Warburton. I make many trips out with Albie, Gary Proctor, Mr and Mrs Davies and Mr Holland – go to Karlkakutjarra to do drawing on the caves near Warburton. When we arrive, we camp there for the night. The next day we go into the cave and draw and paint all day long. We paint the pictures that depict our traditional

Dreamtime legend and stories. When we have finished the painting in the cave we return to Warburton. At Warburton we do painting on canvas using the dot style. We do many paintings.

Once we travelled to Mitika. Mitika is my husband's country. At Mitika we had a meal and then headed off to the cave. It's not a really large cave. It's a small cave. We sat in the cave and painted. Cyril, Mr Davies and Karliwalyku were painting in the cave. These men painted the pictures onto the rock in the cave relating to men's business. We painted all day, only having short breaks for cups of tea and meals. At nightfall we headed back to the camp to eat and sleep. The next day we went back to the cave to complete the paintings. On finishing the paintings we returned to Warburton.

Sometime after the painting job at Mitika we began making artglass. Albie taught us to make artglass. She gave us our boards and taught us how to cut the shapes. We learned to cut the board into our desired shapes and to clean it and lay the shapes around the bowl. Now we do wonderful artglass by ourselves! We do the artglass on our own every morning while Albie is busy doing other things. We have been making artglass plates, bowls for a long time now. Our glass plates and dishes are everywhere in other communities. Today, we still

produce artglass. Currently, all the Warburton ladies are working on a special creation for the new Cultural Centre. Many non-Aboriginal people love our bowls and say that they want a bowl from Warburton.

The other ladies and myself always come here to Albie's place to do dot painting. First, we have to think about what Dreamtime story we are going to paint, then we pick a story and paint it onto canvas. At other times, we go out camping with Albie and other staff members into the bush. There we camp out and sing and dance our Dreamtime stories. Out in the bush we see many lovely flowers and we show the non-Aboriginal staff how we dig for honeyants and hunt goannas and rabbits. We also chop bits of timber to take home for making into artefacts.

We are getting things ready for the new Cultural Centre. Mrs Davies, Lalla, many of the other ladies from here [Warburton] and myself, we have been working for a long time. We will be continuing to make more plates, bowls and dishes.

Together with Albie we are doing a fantastic job! Okay! Next time when you see our work you'll know how it's done and by whom.

That's all that I've got to say.

Tjinyuka (Elizabeth Holland) (Transcribed and translated from Ngaanyatjarra by Lizzie Ellis)

ABOVE: ALBIE VIEGAS AND TJINGAPA DAVIES PUTTING FINAL TOUCHES TO PLATTERS IN THE WARBURTON ARTGLASS CENTRE.

OPPOSITE PAGE: CLEAR GLASS PLATTER BY TJINGAPA DAVIES, *WATI KUTJARRA (TWO MYTHIC MEN)*.

SMALL PAINTINGS BY (LEFT TO RIGHT, TOP TO BOTTOM): SERITA NAPANGARDI LANGDON, RAHAB NUNGARRAYI SPENCER, RAHAB NUNGARRAYI SPENCER, ANTOINETTE NAPANANGKA BROWN, KATHLEEN NUNGARRAYI MARTIN, REANNE NAMPIJINPA BROWN, DENISE NANGALA EGAN, BESSIE NAKAMARRA SIMS, PEGGY NAPURRURLA GRANITES, SHENNA NAPANANGKA WILLIAMS, BESSIE NAKAMARRA SIMS, GLEN JAMPIJINPA JAMES, AZARIA NAMPIJINPA ROBERTSON, HILDA NAKAMARRA ROGERS, FLORRIE NAPANGARDI JONES.

Warlukurlangu Artists
Aboriginal Association

Warlukurlangu Artists Aboriginal Association is located in the community of Yuendumu, 300 km north-west of Alice Springs. The Association was incorporated in 1986 and is open to Warlpiri people from Yuendumu and its neighbouring outstations. *Warlukurlangu* means 'belonging to fire' and was named by a group of women, traditional custodians of the area, including Dolly Nampijinpa Daniels, Rosie Nangala Fleming and Uni Nampijinpa Martin, who began painting by transferring ceremonial body designs to small canvases and dance boards in 1983. Artists Paddy Jupurrurla Nelson, Paddy Japaljarri Stewart and Paddy Japaljarri Sims first portrayed their history on the doors of the local school. This project, known as the

Yuendumu Doors project, was one of the first artistic endeavours to bring fame to the community. Today, artists translate their stories using the modern medium of acrylic paint on linen.

Warlpiri people have a strong traditional culture maintained by story, song and dance. Paintings reflect the artists' Jukurrpa (Dreaming) which defines relationships and connection to the land. Designs used in ceremonial body and sand paintings directly influence the bold and colourful works on linen currently produced by Warlukurlangu artists.

Warlukurlangu Artists is a community-owned and controlled organisation. Over 210 Warlpiri artists currently make up its broad membership and many have contributed to the running of Warlukurlangu's art centre. Paddy Japaljarri Stewart, Bessie Nakamarra Sims, Paddy Japaljarri Sims and Andrea Nungarrayi Martin, as long-time assistant coordinator, have all worked to ensure control of the Association remains within the community.

The Association facilitates dialogue between individual artists and the wider art world. Over the past eight years the artists of Warlukurlangu have become increasingly involved in the production of large-scale commissions for museums and collections. One of the first of these, completed in 1992, was 'Jardiwarnpa', a large 7 m x 3 m canvas commissioned by the Kunstammlang Nordrhein-Westfalen Museum in Dusseldorf, Germany. More recent commissions include the Myer Foundation commission for 'Liwirrinki' and the Morven Estate (USA) purchase of 'Karrku', a large canvas depicting stories from a distinctive flat-topped mountain of that name near Nyirripi, 150 km west of Yuendumu. Separate bush trips are conducted for each of the painting projects, visiting the particular sacred sites that are later to be painted. Several works have involved the collaboration of up to 40 artists from the skin groups connected with the depicted stories.

Large ceremonial ground paintings have been created at venues around the world by Warlukurlangu artists. Installations, prepared with natural traditional materials, such as plant fibre, ochre and charcoal, have been constructed at the George Pompidou Centre in Paris in 1987, and at the NSW Art Gallery during the 1997 Festival of the Dreaming. Warlukurlangu Artists has produced a video, *Warlukurlangu: artists of Yuendumu*, which documents the cultural influences on artists' paintings and some of the major projects undertaken.

Individual Warlukurlangu artists enjoy considerable reputations locally and internationally. Artists are represented in major galleries and museums in Australia and in the UK, Europe and the USA. Works by Darby Jampijinpa Ross, Jeannie Nungarrayi Egan and Andrea Nungarrayi Martin form part of the Australian National Gallery and the Art Gallery of Western Australia collections. Overseas, work is held in the Morven Estate and the Kelton Foundation, USA, and the Glasgow Museum in Scotland.

NGAPA (WATER) **BY DOLLY NAMPIJINPA DANIELS, ACRYLIC ON LINEN,** **91 cm x 183 cm.**

We have been working here [Warlukurlangu Artists Association] since it started. We began painting on doors of the school and the art centre started up after that. We did batik too, then moved on to small paintings and on to large ones. We now do paintings for places all over the world.

We want this place, the school kids come in after school and we show them what Dreamings to do, about their Grandfathers' Dreamings and tell them all the stories about this place. That's how we teach them and that's how they learn about ceremony too, that's how they know about this country. We teach from the little ones to the older ones.

We like to do big canvases, all together, a whole lot of people work on one big canvas with one person as the kirda [keeper for that story]. Sometimes we work here, sometimes we work at camp. Tourists come every month, people fly in and buy boomerangs, small paintings. We make our own decisions and decide about trips to go on and about exhibitions. We set the prices here. There is a committee member for each skin group. We want to keep painting the big canvas, it's good for Warlukurlangu.

Paddy Japaljarri Stewart and Uni Nampijinpa Martin

TOP: *MUNGA JUKURRPA (NIGHT SKY)* BY PADDY JAPALJARRI SIMS, 122 cm x 122 cm.

BELOW: *PARMAPARDU* BY DARBY JAMPIJINPA ROSS, ACRYLIC ON LINEN, 76 cm x 183 cm.

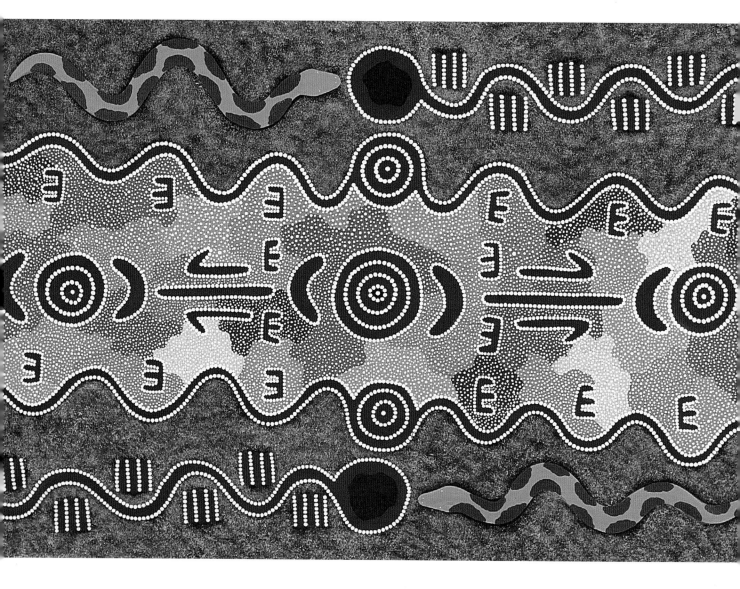

SNAKE, WALLABY, WATER DREAMING BY MICHAEL NELSON TJAKAMARRA,

ACRYLIC ON LINEN, 152 cm x 101 cm.

Warumpi Arts

Warumpi is the Luritja word for 'honeyant' and is the traditional symbol for the country around Papunya, 250 km west of Alice Springs. Warumpi Arts was established in early 1994 by the Papunya Community Council to provide an outlet for the work of Papunya artists and to increase the Papunya community's involvement in the commercial side of the arts industry. The company's goals were established by community elders, resulting in an effective sales and gallery system which returns all profits to the community.

The Papunya community artists have been painting in acrylics on canvas and board since the early 1970s. With the encouragement of a local school teacher, Western Desert painters first translated the motifs of their vibrant culture onto canvas with astounding and well-documented results. Some of the forty artists who are currently producing work for Warumpi Arts have been painting since these early days. Today, the older artists pass on their stories and skills to younger ones who are emerging as skilled artists in their own right.

PAINTINGS AND CRAFTS OF THE PAPUNYA AREA FILL THE WARUMPI ARTS GALLERY IN ALICE SPRINGS.

Many of the Papunya artists who paint for Warumpi Arts have become household names in the national and international art world: Michael Nelson Tjakamarra, Long Jack Phillipus, Paddy Carroll Tjungurrayi, Dinny Nolan Nampitjinpa, William Sandy and Two Bob Tjungurrayi have been involved in numerous exhibitions, commissions and awards, and are represented in collections in Australia and overseas.

Warumpi Arts has its own commercial premises, a gallery in the centre of Alice Springs. This serves as an outlet for the diverse creative output of the Papunya community: paintings on linen, canvas, and boards, carved wooden artefacts, including weapons and coolamons, and necklaces of painted bush seeds.

ABOVE: *KURRINYURRA HAIR BELT DREAMING* **BY TWO BOB TJUNGURRAYI, ACRYLIC ON LINEN, 112 cm x 92 cm.**

LEFT: THE WARUMPI ARTS GALLERY IN ALICE SPRINGS.

It [Warumpi Arts] was set up because we wanted to promote our community's art. It's ATSIC funded and shared by Papunya community. Its future and everything depends on the community itself.

I'm one of the artists and the spokesperson for Warumpi Arts. Liz comes out every two weeks and brings us canvases and paints and comes back in a fortnight to pick up the paintings. We encourage and help the artists to paint. People paint their grandfathers' and grandmothers' Dreaming.

Warumpi [honeyant] is the Dreaming for our area, that's where Papunya is. Warumpi Arts is for the people of our community.

Alison Anderson

ABOVE: THE WARUMPI ARTS GALLERY IN ALICE SPRINGS.

BELOW; *WATER DREAMING* BY LONG JACK PHILLIPUS TJAKAMARRA, 122 cm x 92 cm.

This is my seventh year with Yurrampi. We want to do this professionally, using the right equipment and only doing orders. Otherwise it's a waste of effort. We started off doing T-shirts and bags for interstate and for other communities, but we'll try the fine art prints to see how they go. I worked with Peggy, Lottie and Geraldine; they wouldn't let me interfere with their designs, only to get them on the screens. They were doing really good ones, traditional Warlpiri designs passed on from their ancestors. We did commercial ones too. Kingsley Jakamarra Walker designed curtaining material. We also made T-shirts here for the Tanami Network by Alice Napanganka Granites and Jeannie Nungarrayi Egan.

We're doing really beautiful marbling now, and ink transfer printing, we get the photos and blow them up on a colour photocopier and we put these on the shirt. Nothing's impossible. The fine art ones are used as wall hangings. We can do anything in repeat but we have to find places to produce our work, maybe overseas. It might be cheaper to get other places to make it for us.

At first we didn't know anything. Then we learnt through trainers how to make our own screens and print professionally. We went to Bathurst Island for a look and to get ideas from them and now we have built it up till we have this.

It's good to keep this place for the benefit of our kids and so that some money starts to come back into our community. We're going to get more staff in through CDEP, if the market goes well we can pay them more; it's a lot better than last year. We want to help the council and to help the outstations — it's good to bring it back to the community.

Perry Japanangka Langdon

THIS PAGE, TOP: PERRY JAPANANGKA LANGDON AND TANIA NUNGARRAYI COLLINS IN THE YURRAMPI CRAFTS' WORKSHOP.

OPPOSITE PAGE: A FINISHED SCREEN-PRINT

Yurrampi Crafts

Yuendumu, the home of Yurrampi Crafts and over 900 Warlpiri people, is situated 300 km north-west of Alice Springs. Yurrampi Crafts began in 1990 as an adult education initiative offering the local community the opportunity to diversify their artistic skills by providing training in textile printing and design.

Since that time, Yurrampi Crafts has developed into a small art and craft enterprise that is wholly Aboriginal owned and managed. Currently, it employs one Aboriginal trainer, Perry Japanangka Langdon, a coordinator and an art centre assistant. Previously, Yurrampi Crafts produced an original and contemporary design range of T-shirts, fabric lengths, tea towels and cards designed by artists such as Geraldine Napurrurla Langdon, Peggy Nampijinpa Brown and Lottie Napangardi Williams. These women produced original designs which printers such as Perry Japanangka Langdon, Chris Japangardi Poulson and others transferred onto large screens for printing.

The Yurrampi Crafts' centre is now engaged solely in the manufacture of large limited-edition fine-art prints on fabric. These eye-catching hangings on silk and cotton are printed in small editions on the 20 m screen-print table which runs the length of the centre. The designs, based on traditional symbols, are lively and vivid and developed especially to meet the demands of multiple reproduction. The final product is accomplished wholly on site.

Yurrampi Crafts sells work in shops and tourist outlets all over Australia. Their work featured in the 1993 through to 1997 Central Australian Aboriginal Art and Craft exhibitions at the Araluen Centre in Alice Springs.

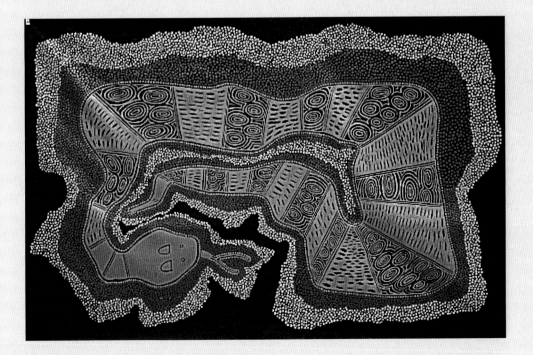

Contact List

AHERRENGE CRAFTSMEN
PMB Utopia
C/- Desart Inc.
PO Box 9219
Alice Springs NT 0871
Ph: 08 8956 9506
Fax: 08 8953 4517
Paintings on canvas
Wood carvings and artefacts

ALI CURUNG WOMEN'S CENTRE
PMB Ali Curung
Via Alice Springs NT 0872
Ph: 08 8964 1955
Fax: 08 8964 1975
Paintings on canvas and board
Textiles: T-shirts, hand-painted fabric and
garments

ALICE SPRINGS PRISON GROUP
C/- 4/4 Mariae Place
Alice Springs NT 0870
Ph: 08 8952 5749
Fax: 08 8952 5749

ANYINGINYI ARTS
PO Box 403
Tennant Creek NT 0861
Ph: 08 8962 2593
Fax: 08 8962 2594
Email: artgallery@swtch.com.au
Paintings on canvas and board
Carved artefacts, painted jewellery, ceramics

APUTULA ARTS
CMB Finke
Via Alice Springs NT 0872
Ph: 08 8956 0976
Fax: 08 8956 0900
Carved wooden animals, bowls, traditional
weapons, seed necklaces
Hand-painted T-shirts
Jewellery, beads

ARTISTS OF AMPILATWATJA
PMB Utopia
C/- Desart Inc.
PO Box 9219
Alice Springs NT 0871
Ph: 08 8956 9506
Fax: 08 8953 4517
Paintings on canvas and linen

BARKLY REGIONAL ARTS
PO Box 259
Tennant Creek NT 0861
Ph: 08 8962 2799
Fax: 08 8962 1380

DESART: ASSOCIATION OF CENTRAL
AUSTRALIAN ABORIGINAL ART AND
CRAFT CENTRES
PO Box 9129
Alice Springs NT 0871
Ph: 08 8953 4736
Fax: 08 8953 4517
Email: desart@ozemail.com.au
Website://www.desart.com.au

ERNABELLA ARTS INC.
PMB Ernabella
Via Alice Springs NT 0872
Ph: 08 8956 2954
Fax: 08 8956 7940
Email: ernabel@topend.com.au
Textiles: batik cottons and silks, screen-printed
fabric, shirts, hand-painted silks, scarves
Wooden carvings
Hand-painted jewellery
Limited edition prints and cards
Ceramics: hand-painted terracotta platters
Paintings on paper, linen and board

HERMANNSBURG POTTERS
PMB 260, Hermannsburg
Via Alice Springs NT 0872
Ph: 08 8956 7414
Fax: 08 8956 7414
Email: potters@topend.com.au
Ceramics: hand-built terracotta pots decorated
with underglaze, with figurines on lids; large
terracotta relief tile-murals for exterior or
interior walls

IKUNTJI ARTISTS
PMB Haasts Bluff
Via Alice Springs NT 0872
Ph: 08 8956 8783
Fax: 08 8956 8783
Paintings on linen, board and paper
Limited edition prints
Publications: *Ikuntji Paintings from Haasts Bluff
1992–1994*, M. Strocchi, IAD Press, Alice Springs

INGKERREKE
PO Box 8244
Alice Springs NT 0871
Ph: 08 8952 8788
Fax: 08 8952 8808

IRRKERLANTYE LEARNING CENTRE
40 South Terrace
Alice Springs NT 0870
Ph: 08 8953 0778
Fax: 08 8952 7794

IWANTJA ARTS AND CRAFTS
PMB 8 Indulkana
Via Alice Springs NT 0872
Ph: 08 8670 7722
Fax: 08 8670 7712
Email: iwantja@arcom.com.au
Paintings: acrylic on canvas
Textiles: hand-painted, silk-screened and
lino-block-printed fabrics
Wooden artefacts and carvings
Limited edition lino-block, screen and solar
prints

JANGANPA
PO Box 2432
Alice Springs NT 0871
Ph: 08 8953 6111
Fax: 08 8953 6111
Email: pyates@vast.com.au
Paintings on canvas and linen
Traditional weapons and carvings
Performance arts and crafts, dance, music, film

JUKURRPA ARTISTS
PO Box 8875
Alice Springs NT 0871
Ph: 08 8953 1052
Fax: 08 8953 1309
Email: jukurrpa@ozemail.com.au
Website: www.ozemail.com.au/~jukurrpa
Paintings on canvas and board
Wooden artefacts
Hand-painted jewellery
Gallery outlet in Alice Springs

JULALIKARI COUNCIL CDEP ARTS AND
CRAFTS
PO Box 158
Tennant Creek NT 0861
Ph: 08 8962 2163
Fax: 08 8962 1924
Email: palace@topend.com.au
Paintings on canvas and board
Textiles: hand-painted silk scarves, screen-printed fabric lengths, sewn garments
Lino-block prints on paper
Ceramics

KALTJITI CRAFTS
PMB Fregon
Via Alice Springs NT 0872
Ph: 08 8956 7720
Fax: 08 8956 7862
Email: kaltjitiarts@bigpond.com
Paintings: acrylic on board
Textiles: batik and screen-printed silk and cotton, scarves, T-shirts, tea towels
Hand-painted necklaces and beads

KERINGKE ARTS
PMB Santa Teresa
Via Alice Springs NT 0872
Ph: 08 8956 0956
Fax: 08 8956 0956
Paintings on paper, wood and canvas
Textiles: hand-painted silk (scarves, wall hangings and silk paintings); screen-printed fabric (off the roll and made into a range of products)
Hand-painted artefacts: boomerangs, coolamons, music sticks, beadwork, mirrors, photo frames, hat boxes and gift boxes
Hand-painted ceramics: bowls and vases
Hand-painted furniture: chairs and tables
Commissions taken for all types of work

MARUKU ARTS AND CRAFTS
CMA Ininti Store, Ayers Rock
Via Alice Springs NT 0872
Ph: 08 8956 2153
Fax: 08 8956 2410
Email: maruku@bigpond.com.au
Website: www.users.bigpond.com/maruku
Wooden artefacts and weapons: spears, shields,
boomerangs, bowls, contemporary animal
carvings
Seed necklaces

MIMILI MAKU ARTS AND CRAFTS
PMB 58, Mimili
Via Alice Springs NT 0872
Ph: 08 8956 7074
Fax: 08 8956 7601
Paintings on canvas
Punu, seed necklaces
Batik

MINYMAKU ARTS
PMB 261
Alice Springs NT 0872
Ph: 08 8956 2899
Fax: 08 8956 7090
Email: aboriginalarts@minymaku.mtx.net
Textiles: batik on silk and cotton lengths
Charcoal drawings, print making, wool products,
baskets, traditional and contemporary paintings
on canvas
Punu, crafts, solar plate etching

NGAANYATJARRA PITJANTJATJARA
YANKUNYTJATJARA WOMEN'S COUNCIL
PO Box 2189
Alice Springs NT 0871
Ph: 08 8950 5452
Fax: 08 8952 3742
Email: mknpywc@ozemail.com.au
Basket and animal figure weaving made from
local grasses, feathers and seeds; seed necklaces

NGURRATJUTA / PMARA NTJARRA
ABORIGINAL CORPORATION
PO Box 8573
Alice Springs NT 0871
Ph: 08 8951 1953
Fax: 08 8952 5958

NTARIA ARTS CENTRE
Hermannsburg
Via Alice Springs NT 0872
Ph: 08 8956 7252
Fax: 08 8956 7822
Paintings on canvas
Silk painting

PAPUNYA TULA ARTISTS PTY LTD
PO Box 1620
Alice Springs NT 0871
Ph: 08 8952 4731
Fax: 08 8953 2509
Email: paptula@topend.com.au
Paintings: acrylic on linen and canvas

PATJARR COMMUNITY
PMB 141
Via Alice Springs NT 0872
Ph: 08 8956 7900
Fax: 08 8956 7609

TITJIKALA WOMEN'S CENTRE
PO Box 149
Alice Springs NT 0871
Ph: 08 8956 0863
Fax: 08 8956 0855
Paintings: acrylic on canvas and board
Textiles: screen-printing, batik; hand-printed
T-shirts and bags
Wooden artefacts
Hand-painted bomerangs, frames, emu eggs and
various artefacts
Handmade greeting cards and mobiles

TJUKURLA COMMUNITY
PMB 37
Alice Springs NT 0871
Ph: 08 8956 7388
Fax: 08 8956 7389
Email: helmaquinn@optusnet.com.au

URAPUNTJA ARTISTS
C/- Desart Inc.
PO Box 9219
Alice Springs NT 0871
Ph: 08 8956 9506
Fax: 08 8953 4517
Paintings on canvas

UTJU ARTS
PMB Areyonga
Via Alice Springs NT 0872
Ph: 08 8956 7029
Paintings on canvas
Silk painted scarves
Carvings and artefacts

WALKATJARA ART ULURU
Mutitjulu Community
CMA Ininti Store
Via Yulara NT 0872
Ph: 08 8956 2537
Fax: 08 8956 2724
Textiles: printed T-shirts
Printed cards
Hand-painted ceramics, decorative chinaware

WARBURTON ARTS
PO Box 71
Warburton Community
Via Alice Springs NT 0872
Ph: 08 8954 0017
Fax: 08 8954 0047
Paintings on canvas and board
Quality glassware for architectural and
domestic use

WARLAYIRTI ARTISTS
PMB 20
Balgo Hills
Via Halls Creek WA 6770
Ph: 08 9168 8960
Fax: 08 9168 8889
Email: balgoart@agn.net.au
Paintings on linen and artboard
Wooden artefacts; beads and baskets

WARLUKURLANGU ABORIGINAL ARTISTS
ASSOCIATION
PMB 103 Yuendumu
Via Alice Springs NT 0872
Ph: 08 8956 4031
Fax: 08 8956 4003
Email:warlu@ozemail.com.au
Fine art acrylic paintings, large commissions,
traditional sand paintings and limited edition
prints

WARUMPI ARTS
PO Box 2211
Alice Springs NT 0871
Ph: 08 8952 9066
Fax: 08 8952 9066
Email: warumpi@topend.com.au
Paintings on linen, canvas and board
Wood carvings and artefacts, seed necklaces
Limited edition prints

WATIYAWANU ARTISTS OF AMUNTURRNGU
Mt Liebig Community
PMB 111
Alice Springs NT 0871
Ph: 08 8956 8830
Fax: 08 8956 8830

WIILU ARTS GROUP
C/- 4/4 Mariae Place
Alice Springs NT 0870
Ph: 08 8952 5749
Fax: 08 8952 5749
Paintings on canvas
Printmaking